Clinical Standards Advisory Group

Back Pain

Report of a CSAG Committee
on Back Pain

Chaired by
Professor Michael Rosen

May 1994

London: HMSO

ISBN   0   11   321887   7

Contents

Published as a separate document:
Annex. The Epidemiology and Cost of Back Pain (ISBN 0 11 321889 3).

Preface

The Clinical Standards Advisory Group was set up in 1991, under Section 62 of the NHS and Community Care Act 1990, as an independent source of expert advice to the UK Health Ministers and to the NHS on standards of clinical care for, and access to and availability of services to, NHS patients.

The Group's members are nominated by the medical, nursing and dental Royal Colleges and their Faculties, and include the Chairmen of the Standing Medical, Nursing and Midwifery, and Dental Advisory Committees. Its investigations are carried out by members and co-opted experts, supported by research units under contract. Financial support is provided by the UK Health Departments, and the secretariat is based in the Department of Health, London.

Remits are set by the UK Health Ministers in discussion with the Group. The first remits were set in 1992, and included access to and availability of specialist services, our report on which was published in July 1993; standards of care for people with diabetes, report published August 1994; and urgent and emergency admissions, our report on which is awaiting publication; and back pain, on which this is our report. Other reports will follow on standards of care for women in normal labour, dental anaesthesia, schizophrenia and the elderly.

Sir Gordon Higginson
Chairman, Clinical Standards Advisory Group.
May 1994

A copy of the Government Response to this report may be obtained, free of charge, by writing to:
    BAPS
    Health Publication Unit
    DSS Distribution Centre
    Heywood Stores
    Manchester Road
    Heywood Road
    Heywood
    Lancashire OL10 2PZ

Executive Summary

Background

In October 1992 the Clinical Standards Advisory Group (CSAG) was asked by the UK Health Ministers to "advise on the standards of clinical care for, and access to and availability of services to, NHS patients with back pain". Although CSAG recognised the importance of prevention of back pain and of appropriate management of patients who do not respond to initial therapeutic interventions, it decided to concentrate on the treatment in the first six months after the onset of low back pain and in particular on the first six weeks in primary care. The report was prepared by a CSAG committee with representation from hospital practice, general practice, public health and physical therapies.

Epidemiology and Cost

CSAG examined the epidemiological evidence on back pain drawing upon the literature, a recent study by the Office of Population Censuses and Surveys and research commissioned by CSAG from Manchester University. Back pain is reported by about 60% of people at some time in their life. DSS statistics for 1991-92 showed 81 million days Sickness and Invalidity Benefit paid for back incapacities, estimated to have risen to 106 million days by 1993-94.

In 1993 there were about 14 million GP consultations for back pain. Approximately 1.6 million people attended a hospital out-patient clinic, a five-fold increase in the last decade. 1.5 million were x-rayed. 1.0 million attended NHS physiotherapy departments. 480,000 attended Accident & Emergency Departments. 100,000 were admitted to hospital and a further 30,000 were treated as day cases. 24,000 had a surgical operation. In addition, approximately 0.5 million people attended for private medical consultations, 0.3 million attended a private physiotherapist, 0.7 million attended an osteopath and 0.3 million attended a chiropractor.

CSAG also commissioned from the Centre for Health Economics at York a study of the cost of back pain to the NHS and society as a whole. It estimated the annual cost of NHS services for back pain to be approximately £480 million in 1993. In addition, lost production costs are very approximately £3.8 billion and DSS benefits £1.4 billion.

Guidelines

In the absence of existing consensus guidelines on the early management of low back pain, CSAG reviewed the scientific evidence on the efficacy of interventions for low back pain, and from this drew up management guidelines. These reflect work by the US Agency for Health Care Policy and Research, the views of a wide range of health care professionals from conventional and complementary medicine and patient representatives who attended a CSAG conference, and "testing" of draft guidelines during visits to a sample of Health Districts.

CSAG found during the visits that the guidelines' standards for urgent referrals were often being met, but that access to physical therapists was variable and generally inadequate, psychosocial assessment was not generally available and that there were long waiting times to see specialists who were often inappropriate for the patients' condition. A multi-disciplinary approach and the skills of physical

4

therapists (physiotherapists, osteopaths and chiropractors) were aspects of the guidelines warmly welcomed.

Recommendations

Recommendations are made for the distribution and promulgation of the management guidelines, redistribution of resources by purchasers, increased support for the management of back pain in primary care, and improved access to physical therapy and active rehabilitation. Back pain should become a key area for Health of the Nation and be a high priority for Research and Development.

Economic modelling demonstrates that implementation of the recommendations should be broadly cost-neutral.

Chapter 1 | Introduction

1.1 In 1992 the UK Health Ministers, in discussion with CSAG, recognised that there were increasing reports of difficulties with NHS services for back pain and a need to consider how these services could be improved. In October 1992 the Ministers gave CSAG the following remit: **"to advise on standards of clinical care for, and access to and availability of services to, NHS patients with back pain"**.

1.2 CSAG appointed a Committee to steer its work on Back Pain, chaired by Professor M Rosen. The full membership of this Committee is given in Appendix A.

CSAG's Aims and Objectives

1.3 The Committee decided to concentrate on low back pain, which is the principal clinical problem and where most of the evidence is available. Low back pain also serves as a good example and model for all back pain. Low back pain and sciatica are considered together. We placed particular emphasis on how standards of clinical care for back pain could be improved, and on how NHS services for patients with back pain could be improved.

1.4 To achieve the aims in the remit, the Committee set itself four objectives:
- to gather comprehensive and up-to-date statistics on the epidemiology of low back pain and disability in Britain.
- to develop Management Guidelines for the clinical care of patients with low back pain.
- to review current NHS services and service developments for back pain in different regions of Britain.
- to make recommendations on the future organisation of NHS services for patients with back pain.

1.5 We focused particularly on the management of low back pain in the first six months and the prevention of chronic disability. There is increasing agreement that early management of back pain to prevent chronic pain and disability is both desirable in principle and is the most pragmatic, effective and cost-effective approach in practice (AHCPR 1994, Fordyce et al 1994). It is also the most likely way to reduce the heavy costs and resources presently devoted to dealing - relatively ineffectively - with established chronic low back pain and disability.

1.6 It was necessary to set certain limits to the task. In accordance with to our remit, we concentrated on NHS services, except in so far as private health care and alternative therapies either impinge on NHS services or may in the future be involved in providing services to NHS patients. The remit did not include primary prevention or occupational health services, although we recognise their importance and their potential implications for NHS services.

1.7 We excluded two related areas of NHS services: spinal surgery and services for patients with intractable pain. NHS spinal surgery is mainly performed for specific nerve root problems and relatively rarely for back pain itself. Spinal surgery is a high-tech, high-cost and low-volume service which poses quite different problems from the low-tech, low-cost and high-volume services for simple backache.

For these reasons we excluded spinal surgery services from our deliberations, except in so far as they inter-act with routine NHS services for patients with simple backache.

1.8   We also excluded services for patients with intractable pain. Patients with back pain may at different times attend firstly for early management and at a much later stage with intractable pain. To that extent, services for early management and services for intractable pain inter-relate. There is, however, a fundamental difference in patients' needs, the goals of management, the resources and services required and the effectiveness and outcome of treatment at these different stages. Services for intractable pain pose a number of very specific and specialised problems, which are presently being studied. (Welsh Office 1992, Scottish Office 1994). We therefore decided that it was better to leave services for intractable pain to others and focus our report on the early management of back pain, both in primary care and in the acute hospital service.

1.9   Throughout the report we have used the term physical therapist to include physiotherapists, osteopaths and chiropractors.

Background★

1.10 Back pain and sciatica have affected man throughout recorded history. The oldest surviving surgical text, the Edwin Smith papyrus from 1500 BC, includes a case of back strain. There is, however, no evidence that back pain has changed. The symptom of back pain appears to be no different, no more frequent and no more severe than it has always been.

1.11 What has changed is how back pain is understood and managed. The symptom of back pain is the common link between a number of serious spinal diseases, the simple backache which most people have at some time in their life and low back disability. Spinal deformities and fractures have been recognised from the time of Hippocrates. But back pain received little medical attention in days of epidemics, famine and short life expectancy. Before the nineteenth century back pain was dismissed as "fleeting pains" or rheumatics. As far as we can tell few people became chronically disabled by simple backache.

1.12 Two key ideas in the nineteenth century laid the foundations for our modern approach to back pain: that the pain came from the spine and that it was due to injury. The syndrome of "spinal irritation" suggested for the first time that back pain arose from the spine and involved the nervous system. The physical pathology of spinal irritation was never identified and it was soon realised that many of the symptoms described in this syndrome were "hysterical". Spinal irritation disappeared as a diagnosis but the belief that the spine was the source of back pain, that the nervous system was involved and that the painful spine was somehow "irritable" was firmly established. The other key idea came from the syndrome of "railway spine". Accidents in the building of the railways during the industrial revolution led to a spate of serious injuries. Public concern led to legislation and the start of the modern social security system. Only then did back pain begin to be blamed on trauma. It is not easy for us to appreciate that throughout history chronic back pain had never been thought of as due to injury. Only with the diagnosis of railway spine was it first proposed that simple backache might be due to minor injury to the spine. The new laws led to a spate of legal activity and medical interest, with many claims for compensation for minor injuries. Once again, no pathological basis was ever found for railway spine and the diagnosis fell into disrepute. But the concept of back pain as an injury and the principle that it should attract compensation remain.

★ Allan and Waddell, 1989

1.13   The nineteenth century also saw the birth of orthopaedics as a medical specialty which was to have increasing influence on the management of spinal disorders. For the first time back pain and sciatica were linked and treated by the orthopaedic principle of therapeutic rest. Patients with serious spinal injuries or disease had always gone to the sick bed, but that had been seen as an effect of the injury and never as a treatment. Patients with back pain or sciatica had never been treated by rest. Indeed, as early as 1743 Sydenham had written "for keeping bed constantly promotes and augments the disease". Orthopaedics for the first time proposed rest as a treatment.

1.14   The discovery of "the ruptured disc" in 1934 provided the focus which brought these ideas together. Only then was it generally accepted that back pain was coming from the spine itself, that it was commonly due to injury and that it should be treated by rest. After World War II there was a great expansion in medical care and social support for sickness in general and in the influence of orthopaedic surgery and neurosurgery in low back disorders. It is from that time that our modern epidemic of low back disability began.

1.15   In 1979 the DHSS Working Group on Back Pain (DHSS 1979) found that "there is a profound and widespread dissatisfaction with what is at present available to help people who suffer from back pain". They also concluded that "unfortunately medical practice appears at times to compound the situation by pursuing policies for management and certification that needlessly prolong the period of incapacity". Since then the problem has become very much worse. There is now much greater awareness of the problem of back pain and disability. It is widely recognised that present health care and NHS services are unsatisfactory and are not solving this problem. It is therefore time for a fundamental reconsideration of NHS services for back pain.

1.16   All industrialised nations face a serious and rapidly worsening epidemic of low back pain and disability (Fordyce et al 1994). Back pain is a problem to patients, to doctors and therapists, and to society. It is a problem to patients because they cannot get clear information and advice on its cause, on how it should be managed and on its likely future effects. It is a problem to doctors and therapists because they cannot diagnose any definite disease or offer any medical cure. To society, back pain is now one of the commonest and most rapidly increasing causes of work loss, demand for health care and need for State Benefit.

Chapter 2 | # Epidemiological evidence on back pain

2.1   Accurate information on the epidemiology of back pain and health care use is the basis for assessing needs and planning health services. Unfortunately, accurate and comprehensive information on the epidemiology of back pain in Britain has not been available up till now. The DHSS Working Party on Back Pain identified this need and lack in 1979 but little has changed since. The Office of Health Economics (1985) assessed the economic impact of back pain but this was based on limited and fragmentary epidemiological evidence. A more up-to-date economic analysis is presently being prepared for the Department of Health (Moffett et al 1994), but was not available when we commenced this Report. It too is based on a limited review of the epidemiological evidence.

2.2   This chapter collates the available evidence on the epidemiology of back pain in Britain, assesses trends and estimates the current impact of the problem, including health care. Much of this material is previously unpublished, but it will be of great benefit to draw widely scattered and inaccessible material together in one accessible package. The review is mainly about low back pain and sciatica, which is at present the main health problem. Low back pain accounts for approximately ten times more disability, health care use and state benefits than does neck pain. Most of the available epidemiological evidence is also about low back pain. The review concentrates on epidemiological evidence from Britain (England, Wales and Scotland but excluding Northern Ireland), although where appropriate this is placed in the context of the international evidence. In general, the findings in Britain are similar to those in most developed countries (Fordyce et al 1994).

Methods

2.3   Four main sources of information are included:
- A review of existing epidemiological evidence.
- An up-to-date population survey of 6,000 adults throughout Britain (Office of Population Censuses and Surveys, Omnibus Survey, OPCS 1993).
- A comprehensive study of GP and hospital health care use by 8,000 adults (Manchester Back Pain Studies, Croft et al 1994).
- DSS statistics on Sickness and Invalidity Benefit for the past 40 years (Waddell & Bryn-Jones 1993).

Review of the Epidemiological Evidence

2.4   A standard search of the medical literature provided background information on risk factors such as age, sex, social class and occupation. Most of this evidence is from international studies. The search also identified a number of earlier British studies from the 1950's and 60's which gave limited information on the epidemiology of back pain and health care use at that time. Only one up-to-date and high-quality study of the epidemiology of low back pain in Britain could be found in the published medical literature (Walsh et al 1992).

2.5   Most of the existing epidemiological evidence from Britain is in the form of reports from Government departments or agencies, professional bodies and other organisations. These are difficult to trace and obtain, and are not widely available. Some of this material is unpublished and is held in the regions or by individuals. For the purpose of this review, further analysis and preparation of statistics were undertaken by the Department of Health, Branch SD2A; the Health and Safety Executive; the Scottish Health Services, Common Services Agency, Information and Statistics Division; and the University of Southampton, MRC Environmental Epidemiology Unit.

OPCS Omnibus Survey (1993)

2.6   The OPCS Omnibus Survey is a multi-purpose survey developed by the Office of Population Censuses and Surveys. It is designed to meet the demand for a fast and cost-effective method of obtaining high quality data. The response rate for March 1993 was 77% and for both April and June 1993 was 80%. Each month, interviews are conducted with about 2,000 adults aged 16 and over in private households in Great Britain. All interviews are carried out face-to-face by members of the OPCS field force of trained interviewers. Survey results are available within four weeks of field work.

2.7   In Spring 1993, the Social Survey Division of the Office of Population Censuses and Surveys carried out a study on back pain for the Department of Health. A series of questions were included in the Omnibus Survey in March and April, and then with some modifications in June 1993. Over 6,000 adults aged 16 and over were interviewed and just over 2,200 people were identified who had experienced low back pain in the twelve months prior to interview.

2.8   The aim of the OPCS Survey was to find the prevalence of low back pain in the last twelve months reported by adults in Britain, and to ask them about their pain. People who reported low back pain were asked a series of questions about when the pain had started and the total time they had had back pain during the year. They identified factors which they considered were related to the start of their back pain. A series of questions covered how the back pain had affected them during the last four weeks including restricted activities, lying down and employment. A further series of questions covered what health care they had received in the last twelve months for back pain ("whom they had visited"). In June 1993 supplementary questions were added about what the GP had done and about sick certification for back pain.

2.9   Material from this Omnibus Survey on the prevalence of back pain in Britain has been published by OPCS (Hickman & Mason 1993, and Mason 1994). Additional analysis and preparation of statistics from this Omnibus Survey were prepared by OPCS for this review.

Manchester Back Pain Studies (Croft et al 1994)

2.10   The Arthritis and Rheumatism Council Epidemiology Research Unit and the Rheumatic Diseases Centre, University of Manchester are carrying out extensive longitudinal studies on the use of health care by patients with low back pain in three areas of Greater Manchester. These include both a community study and hospital-based studies. The community study in South Manchester was funded by the National Back Pain Association and the Arthritis and Rheumatism Council to investigate potential predictors of low back pain and its persistence in the adult population. The framework of this existing study was used as the basis for collection and analysis of additional data on health care for back pain. This part of the study was commissioned by CSAG, as were the two hospital-based studies.

2.11   The basic questions were: "Who attends GPs and hospitals with a back problem, whom do they see, and what happens to them?"

2.12   The community study was based on two general practices in South Manchester. The first

10

practice is in a large council estate with high unemployment, a large number of single parents and elderly people. The second practice is two miles away in a residential area mainly of well-established houses, about half of which are owner-occupied; there is a broad spectrum of social classes and this is not considered a "deprived area". Just over 7,600 adults aged 18-75 are registered in the two practices.

2.13   Conclusions on the prevalence of low back pain in the general population were based on a postal survey of the adult population of the two practices in March 1992. The over-all response rate was 59%. Patient consulting rates for low back pain in primary care were obtained during the twelve month period following the postal survey. Every patient who consulted in one of the two practices complaining of low back pain had a diagnosis recorded on computer by the doctor. The records of all patients who had consulted about back pain during that year were reviewed by a research assistant to obtain information about their care during the three month period after consultation. Details were obtained about further consultations related to back pain, home visits, treatments prescribed, sick certification, investigations and specialist referrals including domiciliary visits. 262 out of a total of 491 patients who had consulted with back pain were interviewed at home by a research nurse during the two weeks following consultation and again three months later to obtain information on outcome.

2.14   Two hospital studies were carried out. The first was based on Hope Hospital, and the second in three district general hospitals in Stockport. Hope Hospital is a large teaching hospital associated with the University of Manchester and has departments of rheumatology, orthopaedic surgery and pain management, all with a particular interest in back pain and spinal problems. These and the department of neurosurgery also serve as regional centres for tertiary referrals. The Stockport hospitals are probably more representative of district general hospitals.

2.15   Patterns of hospital attendances for low back pain were obtained by a survey of new attenders at out-patient clinics. This took place over two four-week periods in 1993: June 1-28 inclusive at Hope Hospital and October 4-31 inclusive in the Stockport hospitals. For practical reasons accident and emergency attendances in Stockport were studied separately for one week in December 1993. All specialties which might see patients with back pain were included: 14 in Hope Hospital and 10 in the Stockport hospitals. A total of 1,219 new patients attended these clinics in Hope Hospital and 1,447 in the Stockport hospitals during these periods. Three months later a research assistant reviewed the case records of all those who had been identified as attending with low back pain. Details were obtained of previous back pain diagnosis, present diagnosis and co-morbidity, investigations, follow-up, tertiary referral and discharge. During the two weeks following their clinical attendance, patients with back pain were also sent a questionnaire about previous back pain problems, current back pain and its treatment, and their satisfaction with hospital treatment.

2.16   Most of the information from the Manchester Back Pain Studies will be published in due course in the scientific literature. Additional analysis and preparation of the statistics were carried out by the ARC Epidemiology Research Unit and the Rheumatic Diseases Centre, University of Manchester, for CSAG.

DSS Statistics (Waddell & Bryn-Jones 1993)

2.17   An annual sample of Sickness Benefits has been collected by the Department of Social Security (DSS) since 1953-54, and is collated in Newcastle. Data on low back pain for individual years have been obtainable but it is surprisingly difficult to access the complete set of data over the years. The aim of this review was to obtain all the DSS data in comparable form to assess time trends. The statistics were prepared and supplied by the DSS Analytical Services Division 1B and collated by Waddell and

Bryn-Jones. The basic statistics are Crown Copyright; responsibility for the estimates, analysis and interpretation lies with Waddell and Bryn-Jones.

2.18 The primary concern of the DSS is to monitor benefits rather than to measure sickness or work loss. Inclusion in the statistics therefore depends on eligibility for benefit. Several changes in the benefit regulations, particularly over the last decade, have excluded increasing numbers of persons from these statistics. Over 40 years there have also been changes in the exact form of the statistics collected. Statistics are collected for both spells and days of incapacity attributed to back pain diagnoses, based on the International Classification of Diseases. Entitlement depends on incapacity for work because of sickness or disablement. Incapacity is mainly based on a doctor's certificate, but since June 1982 claimants may self-certify for periods of up to seven days. Claimants must have paid sufficient contributions as an employed or self-employed person. A claimant need not necessarily have been in work immediately prior to the incapacity, so these statistics may include some people who were not employed prior to sickness. The main groups of people who are omitted from the DSS statistics are young people who have not paid sufficient National Insurance Contributions, those who self-certify for the first seven days and those who receive Statutory Sick Pay from their employer for up to 28 weeks. The recent DSS statistics mainly describe those receiving Invalidity Benefit for chronic incapacity. Most periods of work loss due to back pain are of shorter duration and are therefore not included in the DSS statistics. For all these reasons it is important to make a clear distinction between work loss due to back pain and DSS statistics of Sickness and Invalidity Benefit for back pain.

Findings

2.19 The complete Epidemiology Review and references are in the Annex (published as a separate volume of this report).

Occurrence of back pain

2.20 The frequency of back pain reported over a given period (prevalence) depends on the exact wording of the question. In various studies, between 14-30% of people report some back pain or trouble on the day of interview and 30-40% in the last month. In the most recent population studies in Britain, 36-37% report back pain in the last year. Approximately 60% report back pain at some time in their life, though it is likely that an even higher proportion have had some lesser symptoms at some time. True nerve root pain or sciatica affects 3-5% of people at some time in their life.

2.21 Review of the natural history of low back pain suggests that earlier estimates of the rate of recovery were over-optimistic and over-emphasised return to work. Considering duration of actual symptoms, it appears that 50% of attacks of back pain settle more or less completely within four weeks but 15-20% continue to show some symptoms for at least one year. 70% of people who ever experience an attack of back pain will suffer three or more recurrences but these may tend to settle over several years. 20% of people with back pain (i.e. 5-10% of the population) will continue to have some degree of back symptoms over long periods of their life. 3-4% of the population aged 16-44 years and 5-7% of those aged 45-64 years will report back problems as a "chronic sickness".

2.22 The best estimate of duration of work loss and rate of return to work is shown in Table 1 and Figure 1, presented as a percentage of those who lose any time off work because of back pain.

Table 1 - Return to work with back pain

Days off work	2	7	14	28	60	91	182	365
% returned to work	35	67	75	84	90.5	93.5	95.7	97
% still off work	65	33	25	16	9.5	6.5	4.3	3

Figure 1: Duration of work loss with back pain

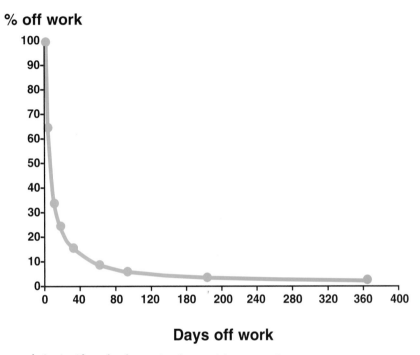

Return to work is significantly slower in those with sciatica but no good figures are available. The longer a person is off work with back pain, the lower their chances of returning to work.

Figure 2 - Probability of return to work

2.23 In considering disability, it is important to remember that all population studies are based entirely on the subject's self-report and there is no objective or pathological information for comparison. Back pain is one of the commonest causes of disability, particularly during the productive middle years of adult life. Approximately 10% of the adult population (30% of those with back pain) report some restriction of activities due to back pain in the past month. More specific and clinically relevant disability affects approximately 3-6% of the population each year. This is also closer to the 3% who report that they had to lie down at some time in the past four weeks because of back pain.

2.24 Estimates of work loss due to back pain among employed adults range from 2% in the past month, to 8-20% in the past year and 25-30% at some time in their life. Actual work loss in employed people in Britain in 1993 is estimated to be approximately 52 +/- 17 million days. About half the working days lost are short spells averaging six days (most commonly 1-2 days) and half are longer term work loss of at least four weeks' duration. The latest available DSS statistics for 1991-92 showed 81 million days Sickness and Invalidity Benefit paid for back incapacities which is estimated to have risen to 106 million days per annum by 1993-94. Less than 10% of this is to people who had been working in the current statistical year. Combining these figures, there was an estimated total working incapacity of approximately 150 million days attributed to back pain in Britain in 1993 (table 3). Only some 5% of work loss due to back pain is due to recorded work injuries but up to one half of all men with back pain and up to one quarter of all women with back pain reported in one recent survey that they believed that their back pain was either caused by or made worse by their work.

Table 2 – Summary of prevalence of low back disability

Disability	Period	Prevalence (%)	
		Those with back pain	Total population
Some restriction of activities	1 month	30	10
Disability ADL > 8/16	1 year	14	5
	lifetime	25	15
Lying down	1 month	7	2.5
Work loss	1 month	6	2
	1 year	20–25	7–10
	lifetime	40–55	25–30

Table 3 – Summary of working incapacity due to back pain in Britain in 1993.

Working days lost	52	million days
– overlap	– 7	million days
Sickness & Invalidity Benefit	106	million days
Total work incapacity	Approximately 150	million days

14

Time Trends

2.25   All the epidemiological evidence which is available shows no change in the prevalence of back pain over the past 40 years. The historical review shows that back pain has affected human beings throughout recorded history and there is no evidence that there is any change in its frequency or nature. The recent change is not in back pain itself but in the amount of disability due to simple backache. This appears to be related to a combination of changed attitudes and expectations, changed medical ideas and management and changed social provisions. Musculoskeletal disorders are now the commonest cause of chronic incapacity and back pain accounts for more than half of all musculoskeletal incapacity. Chronic low back disability is increasing faster than any other common form of incapacity.

2.26   Figure 3 shows the trend in DSS benefits for total days of back incapacity in Britain from 1953–54 to 1991–92. These trends are comparable to other western countries. We emphasise that these statistics do not show an increase in back pain but, more specifically, an increase in sick certification and in state benefit paid for chronic back incapacities.

Figure 3 – Total British Sickness & Invalidity Benefit for back incapacities

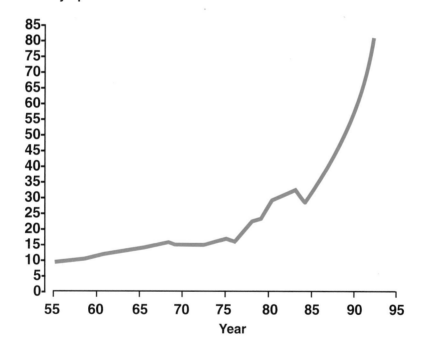

15

Table 4 -.A comparison of Sickness and Invalidity Benefit for back and other incapacities

	1978–79 Days (% of total)	1991–92 Days (% of total)	% increase 78–79 to 91–92
All incapacities	371,041,500 (100%)	573,522,900 (100%)	+54.6%
Musculoskeletal Diseases	60,103,600 (16.2%)	161,107,500 (28.1%)	
Back incapacities	26,380,000 (7.1%)	81,370,700 (14.2%)	+208.5%
All other musculoskeletal incapacities	33,723,600 (9.1%)	79,736,800 (13.9%)	+136.4%
All Circulatory Diseases	56,655,100 (15.3%)	108,570,500 (18.9%)	+91.6%
All Mental Disorders	57,586,200 (15.5%)	105,849,300 (18.5%)	+84.5%
All Respiratory Diseases	53,746,100 (14.5%)	40,399,800 (7%)	-24.8%

Crown copyright 1993.

Risk Factors

2.27 A number of social and demographic risk factors have been identified: age, sex, co-morbidity, social class, occupation - particularly driving, employment status and smoking. These generally influence disability more than pain itself.

2.28 Back pain generally starts between the late teens and forties. The proportion of people reporting back pain increases from early adult life to the late forties or early fifties and remains relatively constant thereafter, at least to the mid-sixties. In those who do continue to have back pain it is more likely to be more frequent or more constant with increasing age. Specific analysis of clinically relevant back disabilities in activities of daily living shows an increase up to age 30-39 and little change thereafter. There is very little change with age in the number of days lost from work because of back pain.

2.29 There is very little evidence of biological difference in back pain in men and women. Women report a slightly higher frequency of back pain than men, similar to most other bodily symptoms. Sciatica is commoner in men than in women. There is conflicting evidence and, overall, very little difference in the amount of low back disability and work loss between men and women. Patterns of work related back injury, work loss and benefit claims may depend mainly on different social influences.

2.30 Back pain is the third most commonly reported bodily symptom after headache and tiredness so it is not surprising that back pain is commonly associated with other complaints. In a recent survey of new recipients of Invalidity Benefit, 53% reported more than one long-term health problem.

2.31   There is conflicting evidence for a relationship between the frequency of low back pain and disability and social class. There is more definite evidence for a relationship between greater work loss related to low back pain and lower social class. The relationship is stronger in men but equivocal in women. This social class classification is however relatively crude and is based on occupation. The apparent relationship between low back pain and disability and social class could be largely related to manual-v-non-manual jobs. There is general though not unanimous agreement that back pain and probably also degenerative changes in the spine are reported slightly more commonly by people in heavy manual occupations. People in heavy manual jobs do lose significantly more time and longer periods off work when they have back pain. Back pain may be more common in people with driving jobs and those exposed to whole body vibration.

2.32   All the evidence suggests that chronic work incapacity and Invalidity Benefit related to low back pain is a particular problem in people over the age of about 50 and associated with early retirement. Although low back pain is one of the commonest health reasons given for early retirement, this is part of a more general social problem and not unique to back pain.

2.33   Many patients with back pain and doctors working with back pain say simply that people with back pain have more symptoms and disability as they get older, and that as people with back pain get older they have increased difficulty coping with a heavy physical job. There are however a number of reasons for questioning that this is the entire explanation. Firstly, there has been a marked increase in low back disability and Sickness & Invalidity Benefit for back pain over the past two decades but during this period there has been no change in the prevalence of back pain and the number of people employed in heavy manual jobs has decreased. Secondly, early retirement because of back pain does not apply only to people with heavy manual jobs. Thirdly, there is considerable other evidence that chronic low back disability is also closely related to non-medical and occupational factors including job satisfaction, wage replacement rates and socio-economic factors.

2.34   There are at least three factors to be considered in the relationship between back pain and disability and work loss. Firstly, back pain may be the direct cause of time off work, job loss, unemployment and early retirement. Secondly, the physical, psychological and social ill effects of unemployment may interact with and aggravate back pain and disability. Thirdly, people with back pain who lose their job may be more likely to receive sick certification and Sickness & Invalidity Benefit.

2.35   On the present data it is not possible to determine the relative importance of these various mechanisms linking employment status, low back disability and early retirement. It is probable that each is important in some people. More than one mechanism may operate together: back pain and disability may contribute to job loss; the physical, mental and social ill-effects of unemployment may interact with and aggravate low back pain and disability; and there may be both social and financial advantages to sick certification and Invalidity Benefit. The social process of becoming disabled and moving on to Sickness & Invalidity Benefit may occur insidiously and unconsciously rather than as a conscious decision. It depends on acceptance by and agreement between patient, family, doctor and DSS. Assignment to disability status, however, may then be almost irreversible in the current economic climate, particularly in older patients.

2.36   There is considerable evidence that low back pain is more common in those who smoke.

Patterns of Health Care

2.37   When considering health care, it should be remembered that many people cope with back pain themselves, without seeking health care either from NHS services or private practitioners. Many factors influence the individual's decision to seek health care.

2.38   Information on health care use can be obtained from patients or from medical records, giving different results. Population surveys generally give higher results based on patient recall and self-report and probably over-estimate health care use. Medical and NHS records concentrate on what health professionals and the health service judge to be the main medical problem, they are often incomplete and probably under-estimate health care use.

GP consultation

2.39   Medical records give very much lower rates for GP consultation about back pain than do population surveys and the true consultation rate probably lies between these two figures (Table 5). Alternatively, the medical records may be considered to give the best medical estimate of **health care use primarily for back** pain while population surveys may be considered to give a better estimate of public **perception of total health care need** for back pain. There are a total of approximately 14-15 million GP consultations for back pain each year in Britain.

Table 5 – GP consultation rates in Britain.

Study	Year	% of adult population consulting with back pain	
Medical record studies:			
First National Morbidity Study	1955	1.3%	
Dillane et al	1966	2.8%	
Ward et al	1968	2.4%	
Second National Morbidity Study	1971-72	5.1%	
Third National Morbidity Study	1981-82	7.3%	
Manchester Community Study	1992-93	6.4%	
Population surveys:			
Consumers Association	1985	14.0%	
Walsh et al	1992	12.0%	
OPCS Survey	1993	16.0%	References in the Annex.

2.40   Overall, the medical record studies suggest that there was a considerable increase in the GP consultation rate for back pain in Britain between the 1950s and 1970s but no definite evidence of a further increase since. The population surveys again do not show any definite trend over the past decade.

Physical therapy

2.41   A summary of the estimated resources and workload of different therapists is shown in Table 6. Contrary to general belief, NHS physiotherapy is only undertaking half the total workload of physical therapy for back pain in Britain.

Table 6 – Estimated resources and workload of physical therapy for back pain

	No. WTE	% of time on back pain	WTE on back pain	Number new patients (millions)	Treatment sessions for back pain (millions)
NHS physiotherapists	12,000	10%	1,200	1.0	?7
Private physiotherapists	2,200	?	?	0.3	1.9
Osteopaths	2,500	67%	1,600	0.7	3.3
Chiropractors	1,000	50%	500	0.3	2.0

Total health care use

2.42   OHE (1985) attempted to estimate total health care use for back pain in the mid 1980s (Figure 4). The best available estimate of current health care use is summarised in Figure 5. The differences in wording in the two figures reflects differences in methodology.

FIG 4 – Estimated annual health care for back pain in 1985 (OHE 1985).

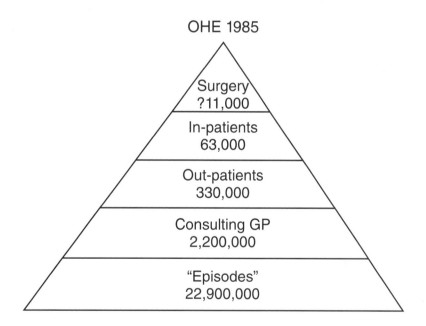

OHE 1985

Surgery ?11,000

In-patients 63,000

Out-patients 330,000

Consulting GP 2,200,000

"Episodes" 22,900,000

FIG 5 – Estimated annual health care for back pain in 1993.

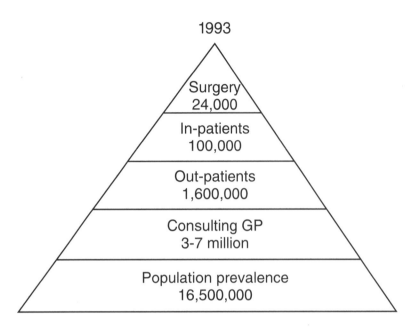

1993

Surgery
24,000

In-patients
100,000

Out-patients
1,600,000

Consulting GP
3-7 million

Population prevalence
16,500,000

2.43   In 1993 approximately 1.6 million people attended a hospital out-patient clinic with back pain: a five-fold increase in the last decade. 1.5 million were x-rayed. 1.0 million attended NHS physiotherapy departments. 480,000 attended Accident & Emergency Departments. 100,000 were admitted to hospital and a further 30,000 were treated as day cases. 24,000 had a surgical operation, a number which has doubled in the past decade. In addition, about 0.5 million people attended for private medical consultations, 0.3 million attended a private physiotherapist, 0.7 million attended an osteopath and 0.3 million attended a chiropractor.

Regional Variation

2.44   There is no evidence of any significant difference in the pathological basis or prevalence of back pain in different areas. There is some variation in the clinical presentation of back pain and disability but greater variation in work loss and health care in different areas. These differences are much greater between different GP practices and probably also between individual hospitals than between geographical areas. These regional variations may depend partly on socio-economic factors but probably depend mainly on physician practice styles.

The Cost of Back Pain

2.45   The Centre for Health Economics, University of York, prepared two economic analyses commissioned by the CSAG Committee on back pain.

2.46   Firstly, they estimated the cost of back pain and health care use of back pain. The Office of Health Economics (1985) previously assessed the economic impact of back pain in Britain in the early 1980s but this was based on limited and fragmentary epidemiological evidence. A more up-to-date economic analysis is presently being prepared for the Department of Health by the Centre for Health Economics (Moffett et al 1994), but this was not available when we commenced this Report and is

20

again based on a limited review of the epidemiological evidence. The present paper combined that economic analysis with our more comprehensive epidemiological evidence to give the best available estimate of the cost of back pain in Britain in 1993. A summary is given below and the complete analysis and references in the Annex.

2.47   Secondly, they prepared an economic model to predict the costs and savings of the Management Guidelines and our Recommendations (Appendix G).

Summary of costs of back pain

2.48   The annual cost of back pain to the NHS in 1993 is estimated to be approximately £480 million (£356 to £649 million). This is made up of:

- 12 million GP consultations at a cost of £130 million.
- Prescribed drugs at a cost of £48 million.
- 2.4 million outpatient clinic visits at a cost of £72 million.
- 7 million physical therapy sessions at a cost of £63 million.
- 800,000 inpatient bed-days at a cost of £106 million.
- 480,000 A&E attendances at a cost of £17 million.
- 1.5 million X-rays at a cost of £45 million.

2.49   Further costs attributable to back pain in 1993 are:

- 0.5 million private medical consultations at a cost of £35 million.
- 7.2 million private physical therapy sessions at a cost of £144 million.
- Over the counter medicines at a cost of £18 million.
- 52 million days lost from work with indirect costs of £3.8 billion
  (Note the approximate nature and qualifications to this estimate Range of error: £2.6 to £5.1 billion).
- 106 million days DSS benefits paid at a cost of £1.4 billion (£0.9 to £1.8 billion).

2.50   The annual NHS cost of back pain in a purchasing health authority per population of 250,000 people is estimated to be approximately £2.2 million (£1.6 to £2.9 million), made up of:

- 54,500 GP consultations at a cost of £593,000.
- Prescribed drugs at a cost of £199,000.
- 10,900 outpatient clinic visits at a cost of £326,000.
- 3,600 inpatient bed-days at a cost of £479,000.
- 31,400 physical therapy sessions at a cost of £283,000.
- 2,200 A&E attendances at a cost of £77,000.
- 6,800 X-rays at a cost of £204,000.

2.51   The annual NHS costs of back pain in a GP practice list of 10,000 patients is estimated to be approximately £88,000 (£65,000 to £118,000), made up of:

- 2,180 GP consultations at a cost of £23,700.
- Prescribed drugs at a cost of £8,000.
- 440 outpatient clinics at a cost of £13,000.
- 150 inpatient days at a cost of £20,000.
- 1,270 physical therapy sessions at a cost of £11,000.
- 90 A&E attendances at a cost of £3,000.
- 270 X-rays at a cost of £8,000.

Chapter *3*

Development of management guidelines

3.1   There is considerable scientific evidence that many of the methods of treatment routinely used for back pain are ineffective (Spitzer et al 1987, AHCPR 1994). There are wide regional variations (Epidemiology Review) which imply a lack of consensus about appropriate assessment and treatment, and that many patients with low back problems may be receiving care which is inappropriate or at least less than ideal. Some patients appear to be more disabled after treatment than before. The trends of increasing work loss, chronic disability, early retirement and state benefits for back pain all demonstrate that current treatment is not overcoming this problem (Epidemiology Review). There is now wide recognition that methods of treatment and management of back pain are less than ideal and that they need to be improved (AHCPR 1994, Fordyce et al 1994, Regional Visits).

3.2   There is growing interest in the development of management guidelines or treatment protocols as a way to improve standards of care and clinical effectiveness in the NHS (NHS 1993). There is both a need and desire for management guidelines for back pain (Regional Visits). There is now a growing body of scientific research on low back pain and disability. Although there are many limitations to our current understanding of low back problems, the existing evidence does allow us to draw a number of conclusions about the effectiveness and safety of many treatment approaches and methods (AHCPR 1994). Several local initiatives in Britain (Regional Visits) and important international efforts (AHCPR 1994, Fordyce et al 1994) are presently developing management guidelines for low back pain. To date, however, no other Government agency or professional body in Britain has undertaken this task. The Committee therefore decided that it was appropriate for us to prepare Management Guidelines as a principal part of our effort to improve standards of care and clinical effectiveness of NHS services to patients with back pain.

3.3   The development of the Management Guidelines was based on established methodology (Scottish Office 1993). This rests on two fundamental principles:
- They should be based on the best scientific evidence currently available.
- They should be based on the widest possible professional consultation and consensus.

US Management Guidelines
3.4   Substantial resources and effort have gone into the development of US Management Guidelines for low back pain by the Agency for Health Care Policy and Research (AHCPR) of the US Department of Health and Human Services since 1992.

3.5   AHCPR set up a research staff and appointed a panel of twenty-three experts to develop the US Management Guidelines. The panel included experts in biomechanical and spine research, chiropractic medicine, emergency medicine, family medicine, internal medicine, neurology, neurosurgery, occupational health nursing, occupational medicine, occupational therapy, orthopaedics, osteopathic medicine, physical and rehabilitation medicine, physical therapy, psychology, rheumatology and radiology. There was also a patient representative. The research staff and panel carried out an extensive review of the scientific literature and constructed evidence tables of controlled trials which met the panel review criteria. Great value was attached to controlled trials which provide the highest scientific standard and quality of evidence. The panel then used this information as the basis for its recommendations in the US Management Guidelines. The full panel held an extensive series of meetings. Additional professional evidence and comment were obtained at open hearings. Drafts of the Management Guidelines were submitted to a wide range of peer and pilot reviewers who were asked to evaluate the comprehensiveness of the literature review, the validity of the conclusions and recommendations, and the practicality of the Management Guidelines in routine clinical settings.

3.6 A member of the CSAG Committee attended as a British observer at several of the later AHCPR panel meetings and took part in the AHCPR peer review.

3.7 The US Management Guidelines are about to be published (AHCPR 1994). The AHCPR Evidence Tables on treatment for low back pain will be published separately as a literature source.

Scientific Evidence

3.8 The CSAG Committee had the important advantage of starting from the final AHCPR Evidence Tables. These provided a comprehensive and thorough evaluation of the scientific evidence on treatment for low back pain up to 1992. CSAG carried out an additional search of the medical literature to include more recent controlled trials. A series of key articles and reviews on the over-all management of low back pain were also identified. This material, together with extracts of key sections of the US Evidence Tables was combined as an Evidence Package (Appendix D). This was supplemented by material submitted by a wide range of professional organisations and individuals from Britain (Appendices C & D).

Professional Consultation and Consensus

3.9 The Committee itself represented a range of professionals involved in services for patients with back pain (Appendix A). To develop the Management Guidelines the Committee devised an additional Sounding Board. Twenty-three professional bodies and organisations were invited to participate (Appendix C). A Sounding Board Conference on the Management Guidelines was held in London in April 1993. The CSAG Committee invited speakers including Professor S Bigos, Chairman of the US Management Guidelines Panel, and 33 other delegates took part, including representatives of the above bodies and organisations and leading British experts in the treatment of back pain, from the NHS, private and alternative medicine (Appendix C). Patients' views were represented by the National Back Pain Association. The Evidence Package was submitted to all delegates before the conference and comment was obtained on this evidence, on the management of low back pain and on management guidelines.

3.10 The Committee then prepared a draft of the Management Guidelines, based on both the scientific evidence and the professional input from the Sounding Board Conference and delegates. Successive drafts were submitted to individual members of the Sounding Board and a number of other invited experts, and modified by the Committee. The final drafts of the Management Guidelines were circulated to participants at all the Regional Visits. Additional comments and suggestions were received at these visits and subsequently in writing from individuals with a wide range of professional backgrounds. Comments were received from a large number of general practitioners throughout the country, and from patient representatives. Individual members of the Committee presented the Management Guideline material at a number of other national and local conferences. The final draft of the Management Guidelines was modified to incorporate as many of these comments and suggestions as possible.

3.11 The final presentation of the Management Guidelines was improved by experts in medical education and by professional desk top publishing. For simplicity and ease of reading it was decided not to include references in the Management Guidelines themselves, but these are available in the AHCPR Evidence Tables and in Appendix D.

Management Guidelines

3.12   The final Management Guidelines are shown in complete form in Appendix B. References are shown separately in Appendix D.

District Visits

Introduction

4.1   A programme of visits was arranged to meet clinicians, managers, members of Authorities and Trusts and consumer/ voluntary associations. At each visit the local service experience of caring for low back pain and the relevance of the draft CSAG guidelines were discussed.

4.2   The eight districts visited were selected to include a range of population size, ethnic composition, rural or urban features, presence of a medical school, and region or country of the UK. The districts were not meant to be representative, but to give a likely mixture of service experience with different resources and arrangements.

4.3   The visits took place between June 1993, the pilot visit, and February 1994 to eight health authorities in England, Scotland and Northan Ireland.

4.4   Between three and six members of CSAG Back Pain Group took part in each visit. In total, 11 members of the Group attended one or more visits.

4.5   Each visit was preceded by the host district completing a simple fact sheet, giving details of the district, service quantity and achievement of quality standards. Information was also provided on guidelines and patient leaflets (Appendix E).

Standards of Care

4.6   Standards of care were discussed with local participants in the context of the following standards:
- emergency referral to a neurosurgeon within a matter of hours;
- urgent referral to a consultant within two weeks;
- access to a therapist within three weeks;
- psychosocial assessment at six weeks;
- multidisciplinary rehabilitation programme;
- very selective referral for x-ray;
- use of local clinical guidelines;
- use of back pain leaflets;
- provision of training for low back pain care.

4.7   Table 4.1 summarises details for each district.

4.8   It can be seen from Table 4.1 that emergency referral and urgent referral standards are met but access to a therapist is very variable. Psychosocial assessment is not routinely recognised as a specific general practice or specialist service. Multidisciplinary rehabilitation was available in only one district. Half of the districts thought that selective referral for spinal x-ray was satisfactory but discussion suggested that there was room for improvement. Xray imaging was recognised to be an inappropriate substitute for a specialist opinion or to overcome unacceptable waiting lists for specialist appointments. Guidelines had been drawn up in three districts but as yet did not appear to be making a big impact. Back pain leaflets were in use in all but one district. It therefore seemed that much effort will be needed if all the CSAG standards are to be achieved.

4.9   There were few examples of active clinical audit although it was recognised that this was an essential process to be built around guidelines with standards. Examples of outcomes suggested for audit included:

*   patient perception of pain relief;
*   assessment of return to daily living, including work.

4.10   The draft CSAG guidelines were well received in all districts and suggestions for improvement were received and have been incorporated in the final version. Some expressed interest in the use of an algorhythm but not all would use it. However everyone thought a one to two page desk top summary for clinicians would be valuable.

Table – 4.1

District Standards	A	B	C	D	E	F	G	H
Emergency referral to neurosurgeons within hours	Y	Y	Y	N	Y	Y	Y	Y
Urgent referral to consultant within two weeks	Y	N	Y	Y	Y	Y	Y	Y
Access to atherapist within three weeks	Y	N	Y	Y	Y	N	N	Y
Psychosocial assessment at six weeks	N	N	N	N	N	Y	N	N
Multidisciplinary rehabilitation programme	N	N	N	Y	N	N	N	N
Very selective referral to x-ray	N	N	Y	N	Y	Y	Y	N
Back pain guidelines	N	Y	N	Y	N	N	Y	N
Back pain leaflets	Y	Y	N	Y	Y	Y	Y	Y
Back pain training	Y	N	N	Y	N	N	N	Y

4.11   Discussions brought out support for other standards to be considered including:
*   GP selected patients to be seen by a therapist within 72 hours
      (selection included factors such as effect on work/lifestyle, and degree of pain);
*   GP referral for relief of severe pain within 48 hours of telephone referral;
*   GP routine referral to therapist within two weeks;
*   all patients to be seen by a physical therapist before they are off work for six weeks;
*   all patients with chronic back pain to receive multidisciplinary assessment before six months.

4.12   There was frequent reference to the 'revolving door' of specialist care for chronic back pain. This included waiting months to see a consultant and then finding that specialty being unable to offer its particular expertise with benefit. A typical example was waiting to see a surgeon for a problem which did not require an operation. The need for hospital specialties to combine their expertise into a multidisciplinary rehabilitation team was much emphasised. There is increasing awareness of the need to provide patients with accurate and up-to-date information about backache and advice about how they should manage it. There is growing professional acceptance of osteopaths and chiropractors and some examples of collaboration between the professions. The techniques used and levels of skills offered by physical therapy services can vary widely. At present, there is variable access to, and availability of, physical therapy for NHS patients with back pain. Earlier referral was reported generally to result in shorter courses of treatment.

Access to and Availability of NHS Services

4.13   Documentation of services for each district revealed considerable variations in numbers of staff and services per 100,000 resident population. Examples are in Table 4.2.

4.14   Table 4.2 shows variations such as few fundholders in District C, many physiotherapists in District F, twice as many orthopaedic surgeons in District B compared with District D. District A appears rich in osteopaths and chiropractors. There is a wide variation in provision of pain clinics.

Table – 4.2

District	A	B	C	D	E	F	G	H
Population	660,000	459,620	750,000	450,000	135,000	646,400	607,522	446,500
Staffing WTE								
GP fundholders	85	29	8	57	6	56	51	67
GP non-fundholders	315	243	500	206	71	338	256	176
Physiotherapists	167.37	167	218	116.05	50	341	180	108.75
Orthopaedic consultants	9	13.5	12.3	9	4	16	8.18	8
Rheumatology consultants	4	9.3	3.3	2.18	0.3	4	2.5	1
Radiology consultants	18	22.6	26	14.82	3.2	29	16.5	12
Hospitals								
District General	3	2	4	2	1	–	2	2
Community	9	–	–	2	–	–	–	12
Trusts/Units								
NHS Trusts	6	3	1	3	2	5	4	2
Directly managed units	–	1	5	–	–	1	1	1
Clinics per month								
Pain clinics	50	28	8	20	4	43	8	4
Direct access physiotherapy service per month★	++	++	++	++	++	0	+	+
Complementary Medicine Private Practices								
Osteopathy	28	NK	14	2	1	3	5	7
Chiropractic	20	NK	11	2	1	5	6	0

4.15 Waiting times for services varied considerably. For example, in orthopaedic outpatients in one district, patients could be seen within eight weeks and in another they would wait 18 months or more. This means rehabilitation is delayed and chronicity becomes established.

4.16 Direct GP access for back x-rays was universal but not so for physiotherapy.

4.17 Rheumatology services have a major role in some districts and quite minor in others.

4.18 Three districts had orthopaedic physicians within the orthopaedic department in a move to make orthopaedic outpatient attendances more helpful for the patient.

4.19 Hospital services provide two distinct services to patients with back pain: specialist investigation and management for patients with specific conditions which require these; and an essential secondary service for those patients with simple backache who do not settle with management in primary care. Many of the present problems with back pain in specialty clinics are due to failure to distinguish and separate these two functions.

4.20 At present, most NHS facilities to treat simple backache are located in hospitals and limited facilities or resources are available in primary care. Notably, District A had a recent development of NHS and private physiotherapy, and osteopathy sessions working with primary care.

4.21 In addition to initial rest, analgesics and physical therapy, a small number of patients with nerve root pain and, more rarely, simple backache, are recognised in districts as requiring further measures for the control of acute pain and psychological distress.

4.22 Domiciliary visits and in-patient admission to hospital for bed rest are sometimes used as alternatives for acute back pain and sciatica.

4.23 The DSS retraining and replacement services are generally reported to be ineffective in patients with back pain.

4.24 Patients with chronic low back pain and disability at present account for 25-50% of referrals to most pain clinics and pain management programmes, although this represents a very small minority of all patients with back pain.

4.25 At present, access and availability for chronic pain services vary widely and there are often long waiting lists for patients with low back pain.

Effects of NHS Reforms

4.26 The panel were reassured that NHS reforms were in general stimulating new and improved services for acute low back pain. There were however reservations:

- competition between Trusts should not interfere with referral between clinicians in different Trusts when these are in the patient's interest;
- communication with the GP of all clinical care events including those involving non - NHS services must be speedy and contain full details of assessment and treatment;
- purchasers need to be more proactive in shaping services through local clinical consensus supported by contract specifications;
- GPs are concerned about work and paper overload under their contract and believe this prevents them giving sufficient time to problems like low back pain.

4.27 Purchasers in the main are not confident about developing a contract specification for low back pain. This is mainly due to the difficulties of obtaining baseline information about a service which is spread between specialties and is not easy to identify. It was notable in the visits that in most centres the purchasers were more keen to tackle areas where 'health gains' were more easily defined and measured, such as coronary heart disease. Diabetes was mentioned as a comparable chronic disorder but one with a dedicated service and measurements like HbA as indicators of control.

4.28 Purchasers and providers need to get together with clinicians as happened with the CSAG visits. They need to review services for low back pain in the context of effectiveness, appropriateness and value for money.

4.29 For the most part, the deficiencies in NHS services are seen to have antedated the NHS reforms. The reforms have the potential to provide mechanisms for improvement.

Other Key Points From Visits

4.30 It was suggested that the system has created the chronic pain patient in the following ways:
- delayed access leads to chronic pain;
- the classic mistake is to give patients painkillers and anti inflammatory drugs and send them home for bed rest without any explanation of the problem;
- bed rest in home or hospital is not the answer;
- patients have been given the impression that there is a surgical cure when there rarely is;
- most commonly, many patients are directed inappropriately to orthopaedic clinics and this is a perception both of GPs and orthopaedic consultants;
- routine rheumatology clinics do not seem to be a better alternative;
- simple backache should be managed in primary care;
- a domiciliary visit by a consultant is likely to alarm patients and is inappropriate.

4.31 The importance of a partnership with patients was stressed in the following ways:
- it is important that patients are helped to take responsibility for handling the problem themselves;
- there is a need to review the information given to patients in terms of style and content;
- time spent on assessment reaps dividends;
- there is pressure on the public to obtain a GP certificate for sickness absence as a means of reducing unemployment figures;
- clinical services should communicate with employers in the case of patients who want to return to work;
- there should be more emphasis on primary and secondary prevention of low back pain;
- some patients with severe pain need very quick access to an outpatient pain relief service;
- patients will benefit if GPs can consider referral to a physical therapist who may be a physiotherapist, an osteopath or a chiropractor.

4.32 Examples of anxieties and concerns:
- doctors are nervous about being sued and this may affect referral of patients to osteopaths or chiropractors;
- patients may demand to see a consultant or have an x-ray;
- the terminology of low back pain has a negative effect and alternative terms such as lumbago, back sprain or strain should be considered;
- better awareness of physiotherapy is leading to escalating demands on the service;

- casualty services may be misused by patients and GPs in order to circumvent long outpatient waiting times;
- physical therapy discharge letters should include details of findings, action and prognosis;
- Asian communities may be unable to articulate the problem of back pain and be reluctant to be examined. Also it is difficult to recruit Asian physiotherapists;
- it is difficult to know which patients to refer to which therapist;
- some GPs wanted direct access to CAT or MRI Scans but after discussion accepted that this was inappropriate.

4.33 New services and approaches which were described as currently working included:
- physical therapists attached to GP practices are reducing hospital referrals. They are able to see patients speedily and outcomes are said to be good. There is also potential for reduction of GP prescribing costs. The physical therapist would take professional responsibility for the treatment he or she undertook. Perhaps most important, the status of the physical therapist must be seen by all concerned as that of a practitioner. At present, some practitioners do fulfil these criteria and there is emerging acceptance of this role;
- as back pain is such a common problem in general practice, a number of GPs are now developing a special interest in back pain, musculoskeletal medicine or manipulative medicine;
- GP direct access to hospital or clinic based physiotherapy can also be achieved with short waiting times. One example suggests about one third of patients with back pain referred for fast access physical therapy;
- GP direct access to acute pain relief services is run by some orthopaedic or rheumatology services.

4.34 Comments on the CSAG Guidelines were consistently favourable and the diagnostic triage into simple backache, nerve root pain and possible spinal pathology was enthusiastically welcomed.

4.35 Some suggestions to improve services for back pain included:
- a physiotherapy service holding open evenings with GPs;
- GPs to be able to prescribe lumbosacral corsets;
- a second opinion service for GPs when patients are not recovering quickly. Such a service requires expert leadership and a range of therapies. Some thought leadership should come from orthopaedic medicine, or musculoskeletal medicine, others that a therapist or GP with special interest could lead the service.

4.36 Improved access to and availability of secondary care for patients with simple backache can best be achieved by a re-organisation of services to meet their specific needs, and at present, the staff, resources, logistics and organisation required are most likely to be available and supplied most efficiently from a hospital service. The service should be led by a consultant. Both patients and GPs expect and demand a specialist service. Many of the resources required for such a service already exist, and are provided to patients with simple backache.

4.37 The need for clinical education was emphasised:
- guidelines will not have an effect unless supported by an education programme;
- physiotherapists, osteopaths, and chiropractors should get together in every district.

Conclusion

4.38   The visits revealed a remarkable consistency of service experience for back pain, albeit with some local variations. All the centres recognised a need to disengage orthopaedics from simple back pain patients, to give maximum physical therapy support to primary care and ensure quick access to a dedicated back pain service, for patients who fail to respond. Purchasers and providers want to improve the services for back pain. The CSAG recommendations should give the necessary support and impetus for change.

Chapter 5 | Development of NHS services for patients with back pain

5.1   In this chapter we discuss the implications for service provision of the findings set out in the previous three chapters, and how future NHS services for patients with low back pain should develop.

The need for change in NHS services for patients with low back pain.

5.2   The Epidemiology Review shows the scale of the health problem of low back pain and disability. This has not been solved by current clinical management or present NHS services. We recognise that individual specialists, therapists and departments do provide a very good service to patients with back pain, incorporating many of the present proposals. Nevertheless, the District Visits (Chapter 4) show that current clinical standards generally fall short of the ideal suggested in the Management Guidelines (Appendix B). Resources are often devoted to symptomatic treatments which the scientific evidence suggests are either ineffective or sometimes positively harmful (DHSS 1979, Spitzer et al 1987, AHCPR 1994, Appendix D). Access and availability are subject to long delays, except for emergency and urgent referral for acute specialty investigation and treatment of serious spinal pathology and acute surgical problems, which is generally satisfactory provided these patients are "fast-tracked". Routine hospital specialty services and referral patterns are largely inappropriate for patients with simple backache. Even when ineffective treatments are not directly harmful they may cause more subtle harm: long delay while awaiting these treatments in itself leads to chronic pain and disability. It also defers the consideration and delivery of more effective management. Overall, there is much ineffective and wasteful use of NHS resources (District Visits, Annex).

5.3   In 1979 the DHSS Working Group on back pain found "profound and widespread dissatisfaction with what is at present available to help people who suffer from back pain". This situation is unchanged today. All the evidence is that this is unrelated to the reforms resulting from the NHS and Community Care Act 1990. On the contrary, in the District Visits we found that the reforms appeared to be stimulating greater awareness of patients' needs. We found some examples of willingness to consider different and novel ways of providing NHS services to meet these needs. Potentially, the reforms provide the mechanism by which this might be achieved. However, it is important that artificial barriers are not created by the reforms. Purchaser specific contracts for low back pain are recommended to overcome this.

5.4   The problems of NHS services for back pain are now widely recognised (Chapter 1, District Visits) and, accordingly, we make recommendations on how these services should be re-organised. Our main priority has been to improve standards of care and NHS services to patients with back pain, although these proposals should also lead to more efficient and cost-effective use of resources. Firstly, we consider fundamental principles for such service. We then apply these principles to the provision of support services for the management of simple backache in primary care and to a Back Pain Rehabilitation Service for those patients who do not settle with primary care management.

Principles of Services for Back Pain

Diagnostic Triage

5.5   Accurate diagnostic triage is fundamental to appropriate referral, to the division of responsibility between primary care and hospital services, and to the recommendations we make for NHS services for patients with back pain.

5.6   Diagnostic triage should be between simple backache, nerve root problems and possible serious spinal pathology (Management Guidelines). Most backache is benign musculoskeletal pain or dysfunction in which it is not possible to diagnose any specific pathology. Less than 1% is due to serious spinal disease such as tumour or infection requiring urgent specialist investigation and treatment. Less than 1% is a systemic connective tissue disorder or inflammatory disease requiring specialist rheumatological investigation and treatment. Less than 5% is true sciatica due to nerve root irritation or entrapment and only a small proportion of this fails to settle and then requires consideration of surgical treatment.

5.7   Diagnostic triage is normally based on clinical assessment, diagnosis and judgement. There is however early research into computer based diagnostic triage, and this may merit further development.

Division of responsibility between primary care and hospital services.

5.8   There should be a clear division of responsibility between primary care and hospital services both for clinical management and for the provision of services. Clinical responsibility for over-all management lies with the patient's general practitioner who should always be kept informed about patient progress. The GP is responsible for diagnostic triage and referral for appropriate care. Management of simple backache is, and we believe that it should be, mainly in primary care. Acute hospital services are responsible for the investigation and treatment of patients with serious spinal pathology or nerve root problems, and for providing a secondary service for those patients with simple backache who do not settle with primary care management (District Visits).

Primary care.

5.9   Diagnostic triage and decisions about referral to appropriate care take place at the point of first contact in primary care. This is generally by the GP, although it may also be carried out by a physical therapist or practitioner. We believe that diagnostic triage is generally accurate (District Visits, Croft et al 1994), and sufficient to form the basis of appropriate referral. It is so fundamental to all our recommendations, however, that continuing education is essential.

5.10   Patients with simple backache who require professional support should be managed, investigated and treated mainly in primary care. These patients have no serious spinal pathology or nerve root involvement and do not require hospital specialist facilities. Recognising and accepting that simple backache is a primary care problem rather than a specialist problem is fundamental to changing patient and social attitudes about back pain. Conversely, public education to change patient, work place and social attitudes is also fundamental to accepting that simple backache is best managed in primary care. The other important advantage to management in primary care is that the GP should be aware of the patient's and family's psychosocial and occupational background and can adjust management, advice and support accordingly.

5.11   Better primary care management of simple backache depends on a fundamental shift and allocation of resources to provide better support services in primary care. It also requires improved undergraduate training and continuing education of GPs in the assessment and management of back pain.

Hospital services.

5.12   At present, patients with back pain are commonly seen by the "back pain specialties" of orthopaedics, rheumatology, neurosurgery and pain clinics (Epidemiology Review, Croft et al 1994). Pain clinics are different from the other three in referral patterns, facilities and practices and will be considered separately.

5.13   Hospitals provide two distinct services to patients with back pain: specialist investigation and management for patients with specific conditions which require these; and an essential secondary service for those patients with simple backache who do not settle with management in primary care. Many of the present problems with back pain in specialty clinics are due to failure to distinguish and separate these two functions (District Visits).

5.14   The first priority of the acute specialties of orthopaedic surgery, rheumatology and neurosurgery should be to provide a rapid and efficient service to those patients who require their expertise and facilities. Unfortunately, at present, necessary specialist investigation and treatment for these patients are often delayed by long waiting lists of patients with simple backache. Acute orthopaedic surgery services should concentrate on patients requiring investigation of possible serious spinal pathology or nerve root problems which are not resolving and those who may require surgical investigation or intervention. Acute rheumatology services should concentrate on patients requiring investigation and management of systemic connective tissue disorders or investigation of possible serious spinal pathology. Neurosurgery should continue to provide a service to patients requiring spinal surgery or the investigation and management of serious or widespread neurological disorders.

5.15   We have already noted that many individual specialists, therapists and departments do at present provide very good services for patients with simple backache incorporating many of the present proposals. Nevertheless, in general, routine clinics in these traditional back pain specialties are not appropriate for the majority of patients with simple backache. These patients do not require or receive any particular specialist investigation or treatment. This specialty pattern perpetuates concentration on disease and on passive and largely mechanical treatment, and creates unrealistic expectations of symptomatic cure. Routine waiting lists for these specialties commonly involve months of delay during which rehabilitation is delayed and chronic pain and disability become more established (District Visits, Management Guidelines). A large proportion of patients and general practitioners are dissatisfied with hospital visits for back pain to these specialties (District Visits, Epidemiology Review).

Personal responsibility for continued management and prevention

5.16   Backache is a common bodily symptom which most people deal with themselves most of the time. There is generally no serious underlying pathology. Medical management should control symptoms and assist rehabilitation, but recovery may not mean the complete absence of pain: residual symptoms may remain or pain may recur (Epidemiology Review). Continued management therefore depends on providing the patient with information and advice, including realistic expectations. Responsibility for recovery and continued management must be shared by the patient and the practitioner or therapist (Management Guidelines).

5.17   There is increasing awareness of the need to provide patients with accurate and up-to-date information about backache and advice about how they should manage it (District Visits). At present, however, much of the information and advice which are given are inaccurate and outdated. There is misleading radiological reporting and clinical diagnosis of normal age related x-ray changes which are labelled as "arthritis". The standard medical advice for simple backache is to rest rather than exercise, and even when advice about exercise is given by therapists it is generally not presented sufficiently positively (see 5.21). There is a general lack of up-to-date, well-designed information and educational material suitable for both patients and the general public. Better educational material should be developed in line with the best available scientific evidence and the Management Guidelines and should emphasise the patient's own responsibility for continued self-care. Public education is required to change attitudes and beliefs about back pain.

Active rehabilitation

5.18   The Epidemiology Review shows that the present problem is not an epidemic of low back pain but rather an epidemic of chronic disability due to simple backache. In the past, backache has generally been managed as a mechanical problem. There is, however, now considerable evidence that back pain and disability are better understood and managed as a clinical syndrome which includes important physical, psychological and social inter-actions (Appendix D, Management Guidelines). Management and advice given to all patients must take full account of the psychosocial and occupational assessment. Some patients will require more specific psychological support and occupational advice.

5.19   At present, standard medical management for back pain is by rest and analgesic medication according to orthopaedic principles and teaching. There is however no evidence to support the use of rest for simple backache for more than 1-3 days, and the ill effects of prolonged rest are well recognised. Most treatments used for back pain are symptomatic, and there is little evidence that they have any lasting effect (Koes et al 1991, AHCPR 1994). Patients do require symptomatic help for pain control, but for a successful final outcome management should also be directed to restoring function by active rehabilitation (Management Guidelines, Waddell 1993).

5.20   An active rehabilitation programme should be distinguished from specific back exercises. Individual back exercises may aim to reduce pain, strengthen muscle groups, and improve movement or posture. They are often prescribed as a second stage of management after pain relief and patients are often advised to stop if pain is provoked. An active rehabilitation programme uses exercises, but its main emphasis is on restoring full function and regaining physical fitness, and is based on progressively increasing quotas of activity rather than on symptoms of pain. The distinction may be compared with prescribing quadriceps exercises for an elderly patient with a fractured femur or teaching them to walk again.

5.21   Most physical therapists advise, prescribe or teach various types of back exercises. There is, however, little scientific evidence to support the value of any specific form of back exercise (Koes et al 1991). There is now scientific evidence supporting active rehabilitation programmes as the best means of achieving lasting relief of both pain and disability (Waddell 1993). All physical therapists agree in principle with this latter approach: indeed, these are the fundamental principles of physical therapy and rehabilitation for all other musculoskeletal conditions. One of the main skills and contributions of physical therapy is in rehabilitation and a few NHS departments provide active programmes for back pain. However, in practice, few NHS patients with backache actually receive early active rehabilitation. There should be a fundamental change in management strategy directed to early active rehabilitation and return to work. It should be based on assessment of the physical, psychological and social needs of the individual patient. This requires change in the medical information and advice given to patients (Management Guidelines). It also requires reorganisation of therapy services and a shift of resources to put the principle into practice.

Time scale of management

5.22   There is clear clinical and epidemiological evidence that the longer the duration of back pain, and particularly work loss, the less successful the outcome of treatment and the lower the chances of getting the patient back to work (figure 2). The evidence suggests that the first six weeks are crucial in preventing chronicity. By 28 weeks, when Invalidity Benefit commences, there is a high risk of continued chronic pain and disability. Current management and NHS services for back pain are generally outside this time frame (District Visits). This is a problem common to many NHS services but is of particular relevance to back pain. Long delays while awaiting treatment lead to chronic pain and disability; if the treatment which is then received is ineffective, it would have been better not to have waited for that treatment at all. A fundamental shift in resources is required to provide NHS services to patients with back pain at the acute stage to prevent it becoming chronic.

Target times for NHS service delivery

5.23 The District Visits have shown a general consensus on target times for good clinical practice and standards of care. These are consistent with the Management Guidelines. Some districts have shown that it is possible to achieve many of these targets with existing resources, modest new development funds and re-organisation. Suggested targets which should be the subject of local agreements between purchasers and providers are set out below.

- *Cauda equina syndrome / widespread neurological disorder:*
  Telephone referral within hours. There should be a locally agreed, named contact for such emergency referrals.
- *Possible serious spinal pathology:* should be seen within two weeks of referral. Direct telephone discussion between the referring GP and the hospital specialist may be of great practical benefit in determining urgency.
- *Nerve root problems not resolving after 6 weeks:* should be seen within two weeks of referral.
- *Simple backache referred to a physiotherapist, osteopath or chiropractor:*
  a) *urgent:* should be seen within 72 hours following direct telephone contact between GP and therapist.
  b) *routine:* should be seen within two weeks of referral.
- *Severe, acute pain and distress not responding to standard symptomatic measures:* should be seen for acute pain relief within 48 hours of telephone referral.
- *All patients with acute back pain* should be referred to and seen by a physical therapist before they are off work for six weeks.
- *All patients with chronic backache and failed primary care management* should be referred for multidisciplinary rehabilitation if they are still off work after three months. They should then be seen within one month. Every patient should have completed a full course of multidisciplinary rehabilitation before he or she has been off work for six months.

Audit and outcome measures

5.24 The main aims of medical management of back pain are to provide symptomatic relief and prevent disability (Management Guidelines): clinical effectiveness depends on the extent to which both are achieved. Clinical outcome measures include pain, distress, analgesic intake, disability in activities of daily living, capacity for work and health care use. Epidemiologically, the most important measure of the effectiveness of NHS services for back pain, and of successfully reversing the present epidemic of low back disability, is work loss (Epidemiology Review). The NHS Management Executive (England) have emphasised the importance of measuring and improving clinical effectiveness in the NHS (NHS 1993). At present, there is very little direct evidence on the clinical effectiveness of NHS services to patients with back pain, although both the Epidemiology Review and District Visits raise serious doubts. Audit is now being implemented throughout the NHS and should be applied to NHS services to patients with back pain. The accuracy of diagnostic triage and target waiting times provide standards for process audit of the delivery of services. Outcome audit is required to judge standards of care and clinical effectiveness, particularly in acute services, physical therapy including alternative therapies introduced into the NHS, and rehabilitation. Audit and outcome measures are also essential to judge the success of the present proposals.

Support Services for the Management of Simple Backache in Primary Care

5.25 Most NHS facilities to treat simple backache are located in hospitals (Epidemiology Review, District Visits). We have recommended that the management of simple backache should be mainly in primary care (5.8). This requires a fundamental shift in resources which should be re-organised as support services for management in primary care, under the clinical responsibility of the patient's own general practitioner. These support services may be located in primary care, provided as direct GP access to hospital services or directly contracted by GP purchasers. We make a number of specific recommendations on how this could be achieved. These should be regarded as a set of options to be selected and adapted according to local needs and resources and patient preferences. Pilot studies will be required and experiment should be encouraged.

Radiological services

5.26 From the District Visits it appears that direct GP access for routine x-rays is now universal and we recommend that this should continue. There is, however, concern about the number of unnecessary spinal x-rays ordered by GPs, hospital specialists and private practitioners. X-rays of the lumbar spine account for 3% of all x-rays. Three standard views of the lumbosacral spine involve about 120 times the dose of radiation for a chest x-ray. There is a statistical estimate that x-rays of the lumbar spine cause 19 radiation deaths each year in Britain. X-rays of the spine in patients with back pain should be carried out according to the Royal College of Radiologists' Guidelines, and these are incorporated in the Management Guidelines (Appendix B). There is no convincing evidence that lumbosacral x-rays are necessary before manipulation. It has been estimated that if the RCR guidelines were followed, the number of lumbosacral spine x-rays would be reduced by 50%. It is particularly important to avoid repeated x-rays when patients attend different departments or practitioners, whether NHS or private, and the radiological reports or films should be made available (RCR 1993, Halpin et al 1991, Management Guidelines).

5.27 Modern imaging (CT or MRI) is primarily a specialist investigation of patients with clinical indications of serious spinal pathology or as a pre-operative investigation of patients with clinical indications for surgery. Because of the high false positive rate in simple backache and some false negatives in patients with serious spinal pathology, the findings must be related to clinical symptoms and signs. These investigations are therefore unsuitable for use as diagnostic screening tests (AHCPR 1994, Management Guidelines). It is inappropriate to use them as a substitute for a specialist opinion or to overcome unacceptable waiting lists for specialist appointments (District Visits).

Physical Therapy

5.28 Physical therapy plays a key role in the management of simple backache. Improved standards of clinical care in physical therapy and improved access and availability to these services are fundamental to improved primary care management of simple backache. We are proposing an increased role and resources for physical therapy in the treatment of back pain, but this is contingent on resources being directed to interventions which have been shown to be effective.

5.29 Active physical therapy of back pain is undertaken by physiotherapists, osteopaths and chiropractors (Epidemiology Review). There is growing professional acceptance of osteopaths and chiropractors. There is also increasing communication and isolated examples of collaboration between the professions (District Visits). There is a need to develop a common conceptual framework and language between medical practitioners, physiotherapists, osteopaths and chiropractors. Common patient information and educational material should be developed, made available to and used by different therapists.

5.30   Physical therapy for back pain has four broad components, although these overlap:
- symptomatic treatment to control pain
- manipulation
- rehabilitation
- education on prevention and personal responsibility for continued management.

These are all important and all should be available to NHS patients with back pain, but the emphasis should be on interventions which have been shown to be effective. At present, the main emphasis of physical therapy for back pain is on symptomatic relief of pain (Jette et al 1994), despite the evidence that many of the modalities used are ineffective (Koes et al 1991, AHCPR 1994). Symptomatic measures to control pain are required but this should be used to embark on active rehabilitation rather than be seen as an end in itself (5.19). To achieve the desired change in the over-all management of simple backache, there should be a fundamental shift in physical therapy aims and facilities to provide active rehabilitation programmes and patient education on prevention and personal responsibility for continued management.

5.31   There is now evidence that manipulation is an effective method of providing symptomatic relief for some patients but again it is only one part of total management (Appendix D). Manual therapy includes a wide range of procedures from massage to high-velocity thrusts and is carried out by physiotherapists, osteopaths, chiropractors and some medical practitioners. Osteopaths, chiropractors and an increasing number of physiotherapists have specific professional training and expertise in manipulation (Appendix F). A number of medical practitioners have also received training in manipulation (Appendix F). Some forms of manipulation are now offered in many NHS departments. The techniques used and levels of skills offered, however, can vary widely (District Visits). Moreover, at present there is no good evidence on which forms of manipulation are most effective for which patients (Appendix D). There is no evidence to support manipulation under general anaesthesia which carries significant risks (Haldeman 1993) and this practice should be discontinued.

5.32   At present, there is variable access to and availability of physical therapy for NHS patients with back pain (District Visits). In some areas there is direct GP access to physiotherapy departments, though sometimes with clinical or logistical restrictions. In other areas specialty outpatient clinics are used to restrict demand on physiotherapy. Waiting times for physiotherapy vary greatly. In some areas patients referred urgently by a GP by telephone will be seen within 48 hours, but this is the exception and only applies to a few patients. Routine waiting times of up to two or three months are common. In a few areas osteopaths or chiropractors are now providing services to NHS patients with back pain. Generally, private physiotherapists, osteopaths and chiropractors see patients within one week. At present more than 50% of patients in Britain obtain their physical therapy for back pain privately (Chapter 2, Table 6).

5.33   There must be a radical reduction in the time taken to provide physical therapy to NHS patients with back pain and resources should be shifted and allocated to make this possible (5.22). This would increase the number of acute referrals for physical therapy. In one region with direct access to physiotherapy, 10-33% of new patients attending their GP with back pain are so referred. However, earlier referral generally results in shorter courses of treatment (District Visits). Increased emphasis on patient responsibility for their own continued management reduces the need for continued or repeated attendance (Roland & Dixon 1989). Consideration should also be given to setting a time limit on a course of physical therapy. If the patient is not clearly improving and returning to work after six weeks' physical therapy (or indeed any form of physical treatment) then he or she might be referred back to the GP with a recommendation on referral for secondary care. Earlier treatment should also, in due course, greatly reduce the number of patients referred for physical therapy at the chronic stage. To a large extent this is a matter of re-deploying existing resources more appropriately and effectively at the acute stage. Initially, implementing the change will require the allocation of modest amounts of new development funding. Depending on local availability and resources, NHS use may be made of osteopaths and chiropractors who will be subject to the same audit as other services. Overall, we envisage a marked increase in the acute NHS physical therapy work load for back pain but a decrease in the chronic work load. This should greatly improve both standards of care and access to and availability of services.

Acute pain relief service

5.34   In addition to initial rest, analgesics and physical therapy, a small number of patients with nerve root pain and, more rarely, simple backache may require further measures for the control of acute pain and psychological distress (District Visits).

5.35   Specialist NHS services for acute pain control are not widely available at present, except for post-operative pain. Domiciliary visits and in-patient admission to hospital for bed rest are sometimes used as alternatives for acute back pain and sciatica (District Visits). There is, however, no evidence for the effectiveness of hospital bed rest with or without traction for back pain (Appendix D). On the contrary, it has harmful physical and psychological effects and is an extremely expensive misuse of resources (Deyo et al 1993). This practice should be discontinued. There is no logical basis for domiciliary visits by consultant surgeons for acute back pain and this should also be discontinued.

5.36   Acute pain relief services for back pain are being developed in some areas, often in association with or linked to chronic pain facilities or acute post-operative pain facilities (District Visits). This service should be generally available as a more appropriate and cost-effective service to patients with acute back pain and psychological distress. Specific resources and referral arrangements should be provided. Patients should be seen within 48 hours of GP telephone referral to a locally agreed, named contact (5.23). The acute pain service should generally be provided on an outpatient or day case basis.

Surgical appliances.

5.37   Lumbosacral supports are of limited clinical value and we are not recommending increased use. There is no scientific evidence that they produce lasting benefits or alter the natural history of back pain or sciatica (AHCPR 1994). Nevertheless, they do offer a safe additional option for short-term symptomatic relief (Management Guidelines). At present, lumbosacral supports and other appliances must be prescribed by a hospital specialist. This is contrary to the principle of moving management to primary care (5.8). The regulations should be changed to enable GPs to prescribe surgical appliances for back pain (District Visits). GP prescription of surgical appliances should be audited to ensure proper use and cost control.

Second opinion

5.38   Some patients and GPs may feel the need for a second opinion, particularly if pain and disability are not settling as rapidly as desired with primary management (District Visits). This may be required to reassure both patient and GP and to provide additional support on:

- Assessment, diagnostic triage and psychosocial assessment
- Further symptomatic control
- Active exercise, rehabilitation and return to work.

5.39 In line with the principle of back pain being managed mainly in primary care (5.8), there are advantages to a second opinion remaining within the primary care setting. This could be provided in two ways:

- **by a physical therapist with specialist training and expertise in the assessment and management of back pain.** There is evidence that many patients consider this a more satisfactory alternative than the present pattern of referral to a hospital consultant (Appendix D, Annex). However, the role and status of the physical therapist or practitioner must change if they are to fulfil this need. Any specialist must formally record and report in writing their detailed assessment, specialist opinion and advice on management. This might be a condition of contract and payment. Responsibility for over-all clinical management would remain with the GP, but the physical therapist would take professional responsibility for the treatment he or she undertook. Perhaps most important, the status of the physical therapist must be seen by all concerned as that of a practitioner. At present, some practitioners do fulfil these criteria and there is emerging acceptance of this role (District Visits).
- **by a GP with a special interest and expertise in back pain or musculoskeletal disorders.** In skills, context and   accessibility such a GP would be the ideal person to provide a second opinion. Although it is important that GPs retain a broad clinical practice, it is now widely accepted for them to develop a special interest and to run special clinics, particularly in large group practices. As back pain is such a common problem in general practice, a number of GPs are now developing a special interest in back pain, musculoskeletal medicine or manipulative medicine (District Visits, Appendix F).

A Back Pain Rehabilitation Service

5.40 Better early management and better primary care services should greatly reduce the number of patients with simple backache who need to be referred to hospital. Indeed, ideally, all patients with simple backache would be managed successfully in primary care (5.8). We recognise, however, that no matter how much primary care management and services are improved, there will always be some patients with persistent back pain, disability and failure to return to work. There is a point at which it must be accepted that primary care management has failed and that further measures are required. If the proposals to improve primary care management (5.25-5.39) are implemented and successful, however, the numbers requiring such services should be greatly reduced.

5.41 We consider that improved access and availability to secondary care for patients with simple backache can best be achieved by a re-organisation of services to meet their specific needs and this was widely supported on the District Visits. This is best described as a Back Pain Rehabilitation Service. It should be a dedicated service because of the numbers involved and the inter-disciplinary nature of the resources required, which cut across existing specialty and directorate boundaries. The service should be clearly distinguished in aims, resources and referral patterns from acute specialty services for the investigation and management of patients with serious spinal pathology or those with nerve root pain who require consideration of surgery.

5.42 In principle, the Service could be located wherever the resources can be made available. Ideally, according to the principle of simple backache being managed in primary care, it might best be located in primary care (5.8). In terms of getting patients back to work, it might best be located in the work place as part of an occupational health service (Appendix D). The question might be one for future research and development. However, the multidisciplinary resources required for such a Service are rarely available in either primary care or occupational health services. At present, the staff, resources, logistics and organisation required are most likely to be available and supplied most efficiently from a hospital service (District Visits).

5.43 The Service should be multi-disciplinary in nature and approach (Appendix D, Management Guidelines), although the exact range of specialties and staff might vary with local needs and resources. Ideally, the Service should have the facilities to provide: diagnostic triage and investigation; clinical, psychological, and occupational assessment; pain control facilities; physical therapy including manipulation; an active exercise, functional restoration and rehabilitation programme; counselling; and occupational or vocational rehabilitation. The main emphasis of the Service should be on rehabilitation and the selection of disciplines and staff should be designed to achieve this end. These needs are mainly low-tech, low-cost and high volume in nature and should be reflected in the organisation, selection of staff and resources of the Service.

5.44 The Service should be led by a consultant. Both patients and GPs expect and demand a specialist service (District Visits). It is also essential for final clinical responsibility and for administrative purposes. Responsibility for the Service should be specified in the consultant's contract, and time allocated in his or her job description. The consultant is likely to be drawn from orthopaedic surgery, rheumatology, rehabilitation medicine, pain management, orthopaedic or musculoskeletal medicine, but possibly from primary care, behavioural medicine or physical therapy. Whatever the main specialty training and contract of the consultant, however, it is important that the consultant's main commitment, responsibility and job description are to the over-all management and rehabilitation of back pain, and not to the provision of individual specialty skills or techniques. The service should be clearly identified and named as a dedicated Back Pain Rehabilitation Service, even if, for administrative purposes, it forms part of an orthopaedic surgery, rheumatology or other directorate.

5.45 Many of the resources required for such a Service already exist, and are provided to patients with simple backache (District Visits). What is needed is more efficient organisation of these resources. Medical specialty input should be largely on a sessional basis, e.g. for pain relief techniques. Osteopathic or chiropractic input could also be on a sessional basis. Although the Service should be consultant-led for the reasons given above, much of the service delivery can and should be provided by clinical assistants with a primary care background, by physical therapists or practitioners and by counselling staff. The Back Pain Rehabilitation Service should work closely with primary care services in the local district and play an important role in continuing education for primary care. Close links will also facilitate efficient referral from and return to continued primary care management. There should be a strong emphasis on self-help to prepare patients for their own continued management. Group therapy and support groups are helpful in principle and cost-effective. The Service should liaise with and co-operate with employers and occupational health services to help patients return to work as soon as possible. There may be links and shared resources with an acute pain service and with community physiotherapy services. The main physical resources required are existing outpatient clinics, physiotherapy and occupational therapy accommodation and relatively low-cost rehabilitation equipment.

Issues for the Future

5.46   This report has concentrated on acute NHS services for patients with simple backache. There are, however, a number of other important issues which we have not considered in detail (Chapter 1). These require further consideration in the future.

Primary Prevention of Back Pain

5.47   There is limited scientific evidence on effective methods of preventing back pain. Further research is required into the effectiveness of various preventive strategies such as safety programmes and training, ergonomics, health promotion, and disability management including return to work programmes (Fordyce et al 1994). There is a particular need for research into effective methods of implementing these in the work place in Britain.

Occupational Health Services

5.48   We have emphasised the importance of rehabilitation for work in the management of back pain and the need for closer contact and co-operation between NHS services, occupational health services and services provided by the Department of Employment and its agencies (Management Guidelines).

5.49   There is some evidence that treatment of back pain in an occupational setting can be an effective method of delivering early treatment, preventing chronicity and facilitating early return to work (Appendix D). At present, occupational health services in Britain are very variable in quality and scope. A few, generally large, employers provide excellent occupational health services. However, only about one third of workers are covered by any occupational health service and most patients with back pain do not have access to such facilities. Retraining and replacement services are generally reported to be ineffective in patients with back pain (District Visits).

5.50   We think that the role of occupational health services and how they could be made more widely available need more study.

Spinal Surgery

5.51   Spinal surgery is now developing as a sub-specialty of orthopaedics and neurosurgery: this requires further assessment and audit. At present the main role of spinal surgery in NHS patients is in the treatment of nerve root problems. Although there is only one controlled trial, there is considerable clinical evidence of its effectiveness. At present, there is no good scientific evidence on the effectiveness of surgical treatment for back pain. Scientific research and controlled trials to test the effectiveness of fusion and other forms of surgical treatment for back pain are needed.

Chronic Pain Services

5.52   If both primary care management and other hospital specialties fail to resolve the problem, patients with intractable pain may ultimately attend pain clinics or pain management programmes. Many of these patients present complex and difficult problems which are resistant to treatment. Patients with chronic low back pain and disability account for 25 - 50% of referrals to most pain clinics and pain management programmes, although this represents a very small minority of all patients with back pain (District Visits). Our proposals aim to improve the early management of back pain to prevent chronic pain and disability. To the extent that this is successful it should reduce the number of patients with intractable pain who require chronic pain services.

5.53   Most NHS pain clinics are part of departments of anaesthesia. Pain clinics and pain management programmes may involve a wide range of disciplines and provide a wide range of treatments. However, most of the smaller pain clinics concentrate on medication and techniques of regional anaesthesia. At present, access and availability vary widely and there are often long waiting lists for patients with low back pain (District Visits).

5.54 Further research and development is required of NHS pain clinics and pain management programmes. Audit is required of the clinical effectiveness of the approaches and treatments used. There should be a review of access and availability of these NHS services.

National Policy

Health of the Nation

5.55 A Key Area in the Health of the Nation (1992) should meet three criteria. It should be a major cause of avoidable ill health. Effective interventions should be possible, offering significant improvement in health. It should be possible to set objectives and targets, and monitor progress towards them. In 1992 it was recognised that back pain was a major cause of ill health and a strong candidate for Key Area status. At that time, however, the Government believed that further development and research was necessary before national targets could be set (Health of the Nation 1992).

5.56 The evidence presented in this report now fulfils these criteria. The Epidemiology Review and economic analysis (Annex) confirm and document that back pain is a major cause of avoidable ill health. The Management Guidelines (Appendix B) and recommendations on future NHS services (Chapters 5 and 6) identify effective interventions which could achieve significant improvements in health. The Epidemiological Review, Management Guidelines and recommendations provide a basis for targets and for methods of monitoring progress towards them. The objectives could be to reduce the incidence of back pain, to improve health care or to reduce the disability which results from back pain. Ideally, back pain should be reduced, but there is no evidence at present on effective methods of achieving this (5.47). Moreover, health care might reduce the duration or recurrence of back pain but not the initial occurrence. The ultimate social and epidemiological effects of back pain are chronic disability, work loss and state benefit and the main aim of the present proposals is to reduce these. In due course, there should be measurable effects on these outcomes. These outcomes, however, are also influenced by many other socio-economic and work-related factors beyond the influence of health care. There are also long delays in both influencing and monitoring these effects and better methods of measurement are required. In the shorter term the most direct and practical method of assessing progress to these objectives is by targets in health care delivery. The Epidemiology Review and Management Guidelines provide the basis for both process audit and outcome audit of NHS services for back pain.

5.57 Specific targets of health care delivery might include:
- The proportion of x-ray referrals meeting the Royal College of Radiologists guidelines and reducing the number of lumbosacral spine x-rays by 50% (5.26)
- Improved accuracy of diagnostic triage, measured by the proportion of appropriate referrals to specialty clinics, physical therapy and the Back Pain Rehabilitation Service, and particularly reducing the number of inappropriate referrals to specialty clinics (5.5-5.7).
- Waiting times and the proportion of patients meeting targets (5.23).
- The proportion of patients with simple backache treated in primary care (5.8).
- The proportion of physical therapy departments providing a full range of services for patients with back pain, including manipulation by trained therapists and an active rehabilitation programme (5.28-5.33).
- The proportion of patients receiving physical therapy within six weeks off work (5.23, 5.28-5.33).
- The proportion of commissioning authorities providing access to a multidisciplinary Back Pain Rehabilitation Service (5.23; 5.40-5.45).
- The proportion of patients attending a Back Pain Rehabilitation Service before they are off work six months (5.23).

5.58 The Management Guidelines also provide the basis for measures of clinical outcome and clinical effectiveness.

5.59 Accordingly back pain should now be included as a Key Area for Health of the Nation in England.

Research and Development

5.60 There remains uncertainty about many aspects of the prevention of back pain and disability and the provision of care for back pain: this should be a high priority for research. There is an urgent need for Research and Development of NHS services for patients with back pain. Considerable scientific evidence is now available, but this needs to be tested and confirmed in Britain. The principal emphasis should therefore be on the implementation of this knowledge and the development of NHS services for patients with back pain.

5.61 We recommend urgent Research and Development funding to evaluate an integrated primary care support system for the management of back pain and a dedicated Back Pain Rehabilitation Service in several parts of the country.

Monitoring change in NHS services for back pain

5.62 The changes recommended in this report should be monitored. The Clinical Standards Advisory Group should review standards of clinical care for, and access to and availability of services to, NHS patients with back pain in three years time. That review should focus on the extent to which the proposed changes have been implemented and their effect on trends of low back pain and disability.

The role of NHS services for back pain.

5.63 Our proposals on clinical management and NHS services should improve standards of clinical care for, and access to, and availability of services to NHS patients with back pain. The current epidemic of chronic disability due to simple backache, however, is not solely a matter of disease or health care; nor is it likely to be solved by improved health services alone (Epidemiology Review). It also involves individual and social attitudes and beliefs about pain and disability, about expectations of health care and social provision for disability (Fordyce et al 1994). The ultimate answer is likely to depend on fundamental change in attitudes and beliefs about back pain and its management and probably also changes in DSS regulations and practice (Epidemiology Review). Changed medical understanding and management of back pain should be the starting point for these wider social changes.

Economic Analysis of Recommendations (Appendix G)

5.64 It is impossible to be sure of the exact costs of implementing these service recommendations. Individual recommendations require additional resources and developmental funding, particularly physical therapy, a Back Pain Rehabilitation Service and acute pain services. There are also major savings, particularly in inappropriate and unproductive use of x-rays, routine specialty clinics and non-surgical hospitalisation of patients with simple backache. Overall, the service recommendations are cost-neutral and it is largely a question of redeploying resources more effectively. The greatest potential saving to society, however, is in the much greater costs of work loss and DSS benefits. Every 1% improvement in preventing back disability could save £38 million in lost production and £14 million in DSS benefits. If we do nothing to improve the situation, total social costs of back pain in Britain are likely to continue to increase by up to £0.5 billion per annum.

Chapter 6

Recommendations

6.1 Principles for the Organisation of Back Pain Services

There should be a clear division of responsibility between primary care and the hospital services (5.8). Management of simple backache is mainly a primary care responsibility. The hospital services are responsible for the investigation and treatment of patients with serious spinal pathology and nerve root problems, and for providing a secondary service for those patients with simple backache who do not settle with primary care management. This depends upon the principles of diagnostic triage set out in the management guidelines. (Appendix B).

We recommend:

The Health Departments should:

- distribute these management guidelines to all General Practitioners and relevant clinical specialties.
- consider them as part of clinical effectiveness initiatives (NHS 1993).
- submit them to professional and educational bodies for consideration as a basis for continuing postgraduate and undergraduate education.
- support the development and distribution of educational material for patients with simple backache and the general public emphasising the patient's own responsibility for care and in line with the management guidelines (District Visits, 5.16-5.17).

6.2 Purchaser and Provider Perspectives

The District Visits revealed a remarkable consistency throughout the country. Elimination of inappropriate referrals of patients with simple backache particularly to orthopaedic departments, rapid access to physical therapy and a dedicated back pain service were common themes. Purchasers and providers are seeking ways of achieving change.

We recommend:

- There should be a redirection of resources currently used ineffectively for patients with simple backache to provide NHS services at the acute stage. This will prevent chronic pain and disability (Management Guidelines, District Visits, 5.22).
- Target times should be set by local agreement for acute hospital specialist services for patients with possible serious spinal pathology, nerve root problems which are not resolving, those who require consideration for surgery and those who have acute pain not responding to symptomatic measures available in primary care. General Practitioners should be provided with accurate and timely information on available services and appropriate referral patterns (5.8 5.23).
- Hospital Services for patients with failed primary care management of simple backache should be designed to meet their specific needs, and be distinct from routine clinics (District Visits, 5.23, 5.40-5.45).
- Services for patients with back pain should be specified in contracts. In the longer term commissioners should be working towards specific contracts for patients with back pain. These should reflect locally agreed clinical guidelines and include standards against which performance can be audited (District Visits, Management Guidelines).

6.3 Support Services for Primary Care

Support services for patients with simple backache should be available as part of primary care (District Visits, 5.25-5.39).

We recommend:

- General Practitioners should continue to have direct access for routine x-rays. All x-rays should be performed in accordance with the Royal College of Radiologists Guidelines (RCR 1993). General Practitioners should not have routine access to CT scans or MR imaging of the spine (District Visits, 5.26-5.27).

- General Practitioners should have direct access to Physical Therapy (District Visits). Local target referral times should be set, (5.23).

- Acute Pain Services should be provided for the small number of patients requiring additional pain control that cannot be provided in primary care. Hospital bed rest with or without traction, and domiciliary visits by hospital consultants, should not be included in contracts (Management Guidelines, District Visits, 5.34-5.36).

- Regulations should be changed to enable General Practitioners to prescribe surgical appliances for back pain, subject to audit to ensure proper use and cost control (District Visits, 5.37).

- Consideration should be given to ways in which a second opinion could be provided in a primary care setting either by a General Practitioner or a therapist with a special interest in the assessment and management of back pain (5.39). This should include psychosocial and vocational assessment (Management Guidelines, 5.24).

6.4 Physical Therapy

We are proposing an increased role and resources for physical therapy for back pain, but this is contingent on resources being used to provide interventions of proven value (5.28, 5.33). Depending on local resources and availability, physical therapy for NHS patients may be provided by physiotherapists, osteopaths or chiropractors, subject to satisfactory clinical audit. Greater professional and academic collaboration between medical practitioners, physiotherapists, osteopaths and chiropractors should be supported and encouraged (District Visits, 5.29-5.31).

We recommend:

- Physical therapy should provide a full range of symptomatic modalities, manipulation, active rehabilitation and patient education in continued management (District Visits, 5.29-5.31).

- There should be a change of emphasis and redirection of resources from symptomatic treatment, to the provision of active rehabilitation and patient education (Management Guidelines, District Visits, 5.30).

- Manipulation should be available as a therapeutic option for the treatment of NHS patients with back pain, and should be carried out by appropriately trained therapists or practitioners (Management Guidelines, District Visits, 5.31).

- Spinal Manipulation under general anaesthesia should be discontinued (5.31).

6.5 Back Pain Rehabilitation Service

Although the emphasis of this report is on the provision of appropriate early intervention which will prevent chronic pain and disability this will inevitably sometimes fail and further specialist services will then be required (5.40-5.45).

We recommend:

- Every commissioner should have a specific contract for the provision of a back pain rehabilitation service (District Visits).

- This service should be provided by a back pain rehabilitation service led by a consultant (5.43-5.44).

46

- Facilities should be available for psychological support and occupational advice. Communications should be established with the work place to facilitate return to work (Management Guidelines, District Visits, 5.45, 5.48-5.50).

6.6 National Policy

The provision of services for back pain is and should remain locally determined, but there are aspects of national policy which have a significant impact on the disability caused by back pain. The epidemiology review and economic analysis confirm that back pain is a major cause of ill health. The management guidelines and recommendations for NHS services identify effective interventions which could achieve significant improvements in health. The epidemiology review, management guidelines and recommendations for NHS services provide the basis for targets that can be monitored. In addition to the Health Department actions recommended at paragraph 6.1 above,

We recommend:

- Back pain should now be included as a key area for Health of the Nation (5.55).
- The Research and Development programmes of the Health Departments and the NHS should evaluate integrated primary care for the management of back pain and the provision of back pain rehabilitation services (5.60-61), in view of the uncertainty about many aspects of the prevention of back pain and disability and the provision of care for patients with back pain.
- CSAG should review the extent to which the changes proposed in this document have been implemented, and their effects on trends of low back pain and disability in three years time (5.62).
- The Health Departments should discuss this report and in particular the findings of the epidemiology review with the Department of Social Security and how the benefit regulations and practice interact with health care and chronic incapacity from back pain (Epidemiology Review, 5.63).
- Consideration should be given to changes in fiscal policy which would encourage employers to introduce programmes to reduce the loss of work from back pain (5.64 and Appendix B).

Membership of CSAG committee on back pain

Chairman:
Professor M Rosen
(CSAG member)
Department of Anaesthesia
University Hospital
 of Wales
College of Medicine
CARDIFF

Dr A Breen
Research Director
Anglo-European College of Chiropractic
Bournemouth
DORSET

Dr W Hamann
Pain Relief Consultant
Guy's Hospital
and
Director of Pain Relief Services
Lewisham Hospital
LONDON

Dr P Harker
Director of Public Health
Dorset Health Commission
DORSET

Professor M I V Jayson
Manchester & Salford Back Pain Centre
Rheumatic Diseases Centre
University of Manchester
Hope Hospital
SALFORD

Ms E Kelly
Superintendent Physiotherapist
North Middlesex Hospital
LONDON

Mr P Lloyd
RCN Adviser
(Occupational Health)
Royal College of Nursing
PRESTON

Miss E K McLean (CSAG member)
Chief Area Nursing Officer
Lothian Health Board
EDINBURGH

Dr C Sears
General Practitioner
SALISBURY

Professor G Waddell
Orthopaedic Department
Western Infirmary
GLASGOW

Appendix B | Management guidelines for back pain

Contents

49

The need for management guidelines

Back pain has affected human beings throughout recorded history and there is no evidence that the frequency or nature of back pain are any different today than it was in the past. What is new is the scale of chronic disability, work loss and invalidity due to simple backache. There is increasing demand on health care and Social Security resources for back pain. Traditional medical treatment has failed to halt this epidemic and may even have contributed to it. There is a clear need to reconsider our whole approach to the management of low back pain and disability.

These management guidelines provide advice on overall strategies for managing back pain. Professional judgement must be used to decide on the most appropriate treatment methods for the individual patient.

The document refers to low back pain but the same principles apply to other regions of the spine.

The guidelines are based on the best scientific evidence now available. The US Back Pain Management Guidelines Panel, set up by the Agency for Health Care Policy and Research, has put a great deal of resources into collating this evidence. These UK management guidelines for back pain have been produced in collaboration with the US Panel and are broadly similar to current US and Swedish guidelines.

They should be used as an outline and may need to be adapted to suit local needs and circumstances.

Figure 1 – UK Sickness and Invalidity Benefit for back pain. The DSS data is mainly on chronic sickness.

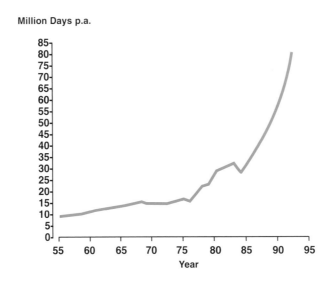

The importance of primary management

The importance of primary management of backache within the first six weeks cannot be over-emphasised. Once chronic back pain and disability are established, any form of treatment is more difficult and has a much lower chance of success. Early management sets the whole strategy and very largely determines the final outcome. It has a powerful influence on the patient's and family's attitudes and beliefs about the problem and how it should be dealt with.

Backache has a good natural recovery rate. There is a 90% probability that an acute attack will settle, at least sufficient to return to work, within six weeks. Hence, there is a clear tendency towards natural recovery. However, the current statistics show that this should not be taken as grounds for complacency, inactivity or a policy of "wait and see" on the part of health care professionals. The good natural history of backache is reassuring, but management must actively support and encourage recovery and act positively to prevent chronic pain and disability. Management must not do anything which interferes with natural recovery; iatrogenic disability must be avoided.

Main aims of primary management

Primary management of back pain has two main aims:

1 symptomatic control of pain

2 prevention of disability

Pain and disability are not the same and should be clearly distinguished both conceptually and in clinical practice. However, control of pain and over-coming disability do go together: they are not alternatives. It is often not possible to provide complete relief of pain and it is not a question of waiting for pain relief and only then starting rehabilitation. Control of pain and over-coming disability must be achieved simultaneously and are mutually reinforcing. Lasting pain relief cannot be achieved unless chronic disability is prevented. The best method of achieving lasting pain relief is by returning to normal activity and to work, even if with some degree of persistent or recurrent pain and with some modification of these activities.

Responsibility for primary management

The main responsibility for preventing chronic low back pain and disability lies with the family doctor, occupational health service, physiotherapist, osteopath or chiropractor who is caring for the patient at this early stage. Early active rehabilitation is highly effective in preventing long term pain and disability.

Active rehabilitation is the key

If the attack has not settled within six weeks, it is at risk of becoming chronic. Statistics show that the longer anyone is off with backache, the lower their chances of ever returning to work (Figure 2). Many physical, psychological and social factors may influence the duration of time off work, but whatever the cause the consequences can be disastrous. Once someone is off work for six months with backache they have only a 50% chance of returning to their previous job. Once they are off work for two years, or have lost their job because of back pain (which may happen very much earlier than two years), they will have great difficulty ever returning to any form of work. They are then likely to remain chronically disabled for many years, irrespective of their further treatment.

Figure 2 – Chances of return to work versus time off work

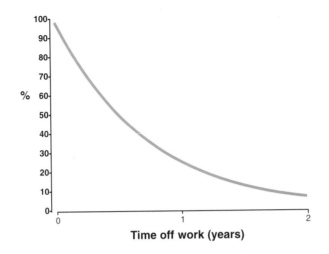

Overview of management guidelines for acuteback pain

Initial consultation

Diagnostic triage
- simple backache
- nerve root pain   ) urgent
- serious spinal pathology   ) referral

Early management strategy:

Aims: symptomatic relief of pain prevent disability

Prescribe simple analgesia, NSAIDs
- avoid narcotics if possible and never more than two weeks

Arrange physical therapy if symptoms last more than a few days
- manipulation
- active exercise and physical activity
  - modifies pain mechanisms, speeds recovery

Advise rest only if essential: 1–3 days
- prolonged bed rest is harmful

Encourage early activity
- activity is not harmful
- reduces pain
- physical fitness beneficial

Practise psychosocial management; this is fundamental
- promote positive attitudes to activity and work
- distress and depression

Advise absence from work only if unavoidable; early return to work
- prolonged sickness absence makes return to work increasingly difficult

Biopsychosocial assessment at 6 weeks

Review diagnostic triage

ESR and x-ray lumbosacral spine if specifically indicated

Psychosocial and vocational assessment

Active rehabilitation programme

Incremental aerobic exercise and fitness programme of physical reconditioning

Behavioural medicine principles

Close liaison with the workplace

Secondary referral

Second opinion

Rehabilitation

Vocational assessment and guidance

Surgery

Pain management

Final outcome measure: maintain productive activity; reduce work loss

Diagnostic triage

A careful history and physical examination is essential in establishing rapport with the patient and providing reassurance and understanding of the best management strategy for simple backache. The first step in diagnosis is to determine that this is a musculoskeletal problem and to exclude non-spinal pathology such as renal, abdominal or gynaecological disease. The musculoskeletal assessment should then exclude serious spinal pathology, and should distinguish a nerve root problem from simple backache.

Diagnostic Triage - simple backache
         - nerve root pain
         - possible serious spinal pathology

The term simple backache has been used to describe the common "mechanical" back pain which is musculoskeletal in origin and in which symptoms vary with different physical activities. Pain receptors are present in bone, joints, muscle, connective tissue, periosteum, the outer third of the intervertebral disc and in perivascular tissue. Pain receptors may be activated by mechanical strain, metabolites or inflammation. Clinically, simple backache is commonly related to mechanical strain or dysfunction although it often appears to develop spontaneously. Simple backache may be very painful and often spreads as referred leg pain to one or both hips or thighs. However, the term simple backache also provides reassurance that the nerve roots and spinal cord are not compromised and that there is no evidence of more serious spinal pathology such as tumour or infection. Attempts at more precise diagnosis of simple backache based on theories of aetiology or pathology are not generally agreed by different specialties and tend to be unhelpful when deciding on management.

The term nerve root pain has been used in preference to sciatica to emphasise its underlying pathological basis and specific clinical features. Nerve root pain is commonly caused by a disc prolapse, spinal stenosis or surgical scarring. Permanent damage to the nervous system itself may also give rise to neuropathic pain. Nerve root pain commonly arises from a single nerve root and when more than one nerve root appears to be involved then a more widespread neurological disorder should be considered. In contrast to the referred leg pain described above, nerve root pain is relatively well localised, unilateral leg pain which at least approximates to a dermatomal distribution and commonly radiates into the foot or toes. It is often associated with numbness or paraesthesia in the same distribution. There may be specific signs of nerve irritation or localised motor, sensory or reflex signs of nerve root compression affecting the same dermatomal or myotomal distribution, though these are not essential for the diagnosis. When present, nerve root pain is usually the dominant clinical presentation.

The term serious spinal pathology has been used to include spinal tumour and infection, inflammatory disease such as ankylosing spondylitis, structural deformity such as scoliosis, and widespread neurological disorders. These may produce back pain or less commonly nerve root pain. The back pain is often constant, progressive and "non-mechanical" in that it is unrelated to physical activity, although if structural failure occurs then mechanical back pain may also be produced. The major clinical presentation, diagnosis and management, however, concern the underlying spinal pathology.

The diagnostic triage forms the basis for decisions about referral, investigation and further management. It largely determines the further course and final outcome of treatment. Any errors in the initial diagnostic triage may have serious consequences.

Although the history must be thorough, if it is carefully focused on the following key elements it can be carried out within the average GP consultation time of nine minutes. The main purpose of a brief examination is to check or corroborate the history, and should focus on specific signs of nerve root involvement or neurological compromise.

The main diagnostic indicators for simple backache, nerve root pain, "red flags", cauda equina syndrome/widespread neurological disorder, and inflammatory disorders are outlined below:

SIMPLE BACKACHE

Onset generally age 20-55 years

Lumbosacral region, buttocks and thighs

Pain "mechanical" in nature
 - varies with physical activity
 - varies with time

Patient well

Prognosis good
 - 90% recover from acute attack in six

RED FLAGS

Possible Serious Spinal pathology

Age of onset < 20 or > 55 years

Violent Trauma: eg fall from a height, RTA

Constant, progressive, non-mechanical pain

Thoracic pain

PMH - Carcinoma

Systemic steroids

Drug abuse, HIV

Systemically unwell

Weight loss

Persisting severe restriction of lumbar flexion

Widespread neurology

Structural deformity

If there are suspicious clinical features or if pain has not settled in 6 weeks, an ESR and plain X-ray should be considered.

NERVE ROOT PAIN

Unilateral leg pain > back pain

Pain generally radiates to foot or toes

Numbness and paraesthesia in the same distribution

Nerve irritation signs
 - reduced SLR which reproduces leg pain

Motor, sensory or reflex change
 - limited to one nerve root

Prognosis reasonable
 - 50% recover from acute attack within six weeks

CAUDA EQUINA SYNDROME/WIDESPREAD NEUROLOGICAL DISORDER

Difficulty with micturition

Loss of anal sphincter tone or faecal incontinence

Saddle anaesthesia about the anus, perineum or genitals

Widespread (>one nerve root) or progressive motor weakness in the legs or gait disturbance

INFLAMMATORY DISORDERS

(Ankylosing spondylitis and related disorders)

Gradual onset

Marked morning stiffness

Persisting limitation spinal movements in all directions

Peripheral joint involvement

Iritis, skin rashes (psoriasis), colitis, urethral discharge

Family history

Emergency and urgent referrals

The initial diagnostic triage will identify the small number of patients requiring urgent and emergency referral to a hospital specialist. Guidelines for emergency and urgent referrals are set out below.

Emergency referral:

Diagnosis: Acute spinal cord damage/acute cauda equina syndrome/widespread neurological disorder.

Action: Emergency referral to a specialist with experience in spinal surgery within a matter of hours.

Urgent referrals (within a few weeks):

Diagnosis: Possible serious spinal pathology.

Action: Urgent referral for specialist investigation, generally to an orthopaedic surgeon or rheumatologist, depending on local availability.

Diagnosis: Possible acute inflammatory disorders.

Action: Urgent referral to a rheumatologist.

Diagnosis: Nerve root problem.

Action: Should generally be dealt with initially by the GP, providing there is no major or progressive motor weakness. Early referral may be required for additional acute pain control. If it is not resolving satisfactorily after six weeks, the patient should then be referred urgently for appropriate specialist assessment and investigation.

Summary: Diagnostic Triage and Referral

	Initial management	If not reshowing by 4-6 weeks
Possible serious spinal pathology	Urgent/emergency referral for Specialist investigation	
Nerve root problem	General practitioner ? Refer for acute pain control ? Physiotherapy ?? Osteopathy/Chiropractic	Urgent surgical referral
Simple backache	General practitioner ? Physiotherapy ? Osteopathy/Chiropractic ?? Refer for acute pain control	Psychosocial & vocational assessment Active rehabilitation for return to work

Diagnostic Imaging

X-rays should be used as advised in the Royal College of Radiologists guidelines.

No routine need for x-ray

Unnecessary irradiation should be avoided. Standard x-rays of the lumbosacral spine involve about 120 times the dose of radiation for a chest x-ray. X-rays are not usually required in the initial management of acute back pain in patients between the ages of 20 and 55 years. Acute back pain is usually caused by conditions which cannot be diagnosed by plain x-rays. Pain correlates poorly with degenerative changes found on x-rays: these x-ray findings are usually normal, age-related changes and should not be labelled "arthritis".

When to arrange x-rays

AP and lateral x-rays of the lumbosacral spine are required if there is a question of possible serious spinal pathology. If thoracic pain is present, thoracic x-rays may also be required. X-rays of the lumbo-sacral spine may be performed for simple backache if symptoms and disability are not improving after six weeks. It should always be remembered that lumbar spinal radiography involves one of the highest radiation doses of any plain radiographic procedure, and that the yield of positive findings is very low.

What x-rays cannot show

It is important to remember that serious pathology can exist in the presence of normal x-rays. It takes time for such disease processes to produce bony destruction and false negative x-rays are common in the early stages of both tumour and infection. If there are clinical "red flags" of possible serious spinal pathology, then a negative x-ray does not exclude infection or tumour and referral and investigation should proceed.

X-rays should not delay urgent referral

If the patient is being referred urgently for specialist investigation, it may be better to let the specialist arrange the necessary x-rays. Referral should not be delayed while awaiting x-rays.

Other Imaging Techniques

Diagnostic imaging with CT or MRI provides detailed anatomical information of serious spinal pathology and for the pre-operative planning of nerve root problems. Their use in simple backache is less well established. Because of their high false positive rates due to normal age related changes they are not suitable for diagnostic screening.

After comprehensive clinical assessment and plain x-rays, a bone scan may provide a better second line test for serious spinal pathology.

Primary management of simple backache

Most acute backache is probably of soft tissue origin. Although it is often not possible to identify the exact origin of the pain, there is now good evidence on which to base the musculoskeletal principles of management.

Information and advice

There is general agreement that patients should be given accurate information about back pain and about the structure and function of the back. Avoid serious labels like "arthritis of the spine"; reassure the patient that age related x-ray changes are normal. Medical information and advice may have lasting effects on the patient's and family's attitudes and beliefs about the problem and how it should be managed. This information and advice should be designed to reduce apprehension and encourage progressive mobilisation and rehabilitation.

Patients should be given simple, practical advice on how to avoid excessive loads on the back while performing everyday activities. Advice should be tailored to the patient's individual life and work. Three key areas of information to cover are:
- expectations about rapid recovery but also possible recurrence of symptoms.
- safe and proven methods of symptom control.
- safe and reasonable activity modifications.

Responsibility for management

Most acute and recurrent episodes of simple backache are managed by the person themself or by the GP. Primary management may also commonly involve an occupational health service or a physiotherapist, osteopath or chiropractor. Hospital specialist referral is generally neither required nor helpful.

Recurrence of simple backache

The history, examination and initial diagnostic triage provide the basis for reassurance that the patient's condition is simple backache with no evidence of a trapped nerve or of any more serious underlying pathology. Simple backache should be a benign, self-limiting condition.

However, while 90% of acute or recurrent attacks settle within six weeks, 60% of people may have at least one recurrence within the next year. These recurrent attacks may become nearly as much a cause for clinical concern and work loss as chronic pain. Recurrent attacks do tend to settle over three to five years, but frequent recurrence may require secondary referral and management similar to chronic pain.

Age and simple backache

Patients should be reassured that back pain does not generally increase with age. Simple backache generally peaks in the middle decades of life and tends to become less frequent in later life.

Early management strategy

There is increasing evidence that the approach outlined below improves the natural history of simple backache and reduces recurrence. On the available evidence the best early management strategy consists of:

Prescribe simple analgesia, NSAIDS
- avoid narcotics if possible and never for more than two weeks

Arrange physical therapy if symptoms last more than a few days
- manipulation
- active exercise and physical activity
  - modifies pain and mechanisms, speeds recovery

Advise rest only if essential: one to three days maximum

- prolonged bed rest is harmful

Encourage early activity

- activity is not harmful
- reduces pain
- physical fitness beneficial

Practise psychosocial management, this is fundamental

- promote positive attitudes to activity and work
- awareness and management of distress and depression

Avoiding loss of work

The most important consequence of backache is loss of time from work and even loss of employment. The aim of management must be to maintain productive activity and minimise work loss. Back pain may restrict physical activity and activities may need to be modified at the acute stage. However, it is important to avoid iatrogenic disability.

Whenever possible, every effort should be made to keep the patient at work. Symptomatic measures to control pain should be used to help the patient stay active. Simple, practical advice should be given on how to modify physical activities. If an occupational health service is available it may be able to assist at work. A patient at work should not be advised to stop work except on the rare occasion when there is clear evidence that remaining at work is likely to cause lasting physical harm. There is rarely any clear clinical basis for advising a patient to change their job or to give up work because of simple backache. The consequences of medical advice about work must be considered very carefully and discussed in detail with the patient.

The prognosis for successful treatment and rehabilitation is poorer in patients who are unemployed or who have lost their job due to back pain. Management should then concentrate on providing symptomatic relief and on restoration of physical activity levels and whatever form of productive activity is available to the patient. However, medical treatment cannot solve the social problems of unemployment and it is important to avoid medicalising the problem and adding all the long term consequences of assignment to invalidity status.

Managing nerve root pain

Most acute episodes of nerve root pain resolve naturally without requiring surgery. For the first six weeks management follows the same principles as simple backache, but progress is likely to be slower. Adequate analgesia is particularly important initially. A higher proportion of patients may require initial bed rest which may be required for up to one or two weeks. There is no evidence to support bed rest for more than two weeks even for severe nerve root pain, but the harmful effects of more prolonged bed rest are well recognised in standard medical and nursing teaching. Mobilisation and rehabilitation then follow the same principles as simple backache but progress is generally slower.

Symptomatic measures

a) Medication

Simple analgesics are adequate for most patients. Medication should be given on a regular basis for a fixed duration to control pain, and not intermittently p.r.n.

Guidelines for medication are:

- Paracetamol up to 4g per day in divided doses

- If inadequate on its own, paracetamol may be used in combination tablets with codeine (Co-codamol), dihydrocodeine (Co-dydramol) or dextropropoxyphene (Co-proxamol).

- Non-steroidal anti-inflammatory drugs (NSAIDs) may be used, particularly if there is marked stiffness. The simplest and safest NSAID is ibuprofen. Aspirin is still a useful alternative. NSAIDs should be avoided if the patient has dyspepsia, or may be combined with anti-ulcer treatment. When there is marked muscle spasm, analgesics or NSAIDs may be combined with a muscle relaxant such as methocarbamol or baclophen.

- When there is marked psychological distress, analgesics or NSAIDs may be combined with a sedative such as benzodiazepine (Diazepam). These should generally only be used for short periods and are rarely required for more than two weeks.

- Narcotics such as morphine and pethidine are only rarely indicated and generally only for a few days. Opioid derivatives or alternatives such as Meptazinol, Nefopam, Bupramorphine or Pentazocine may be considered instead for short periods. If any of these drugs are required for more than two weeks, urgent specialist opinion should be sought.

b) Manipulation

There is considerable evidence that manipulation can provide short-term symptomatic benefit in some patients with acute back pain of less than one month's duration and without nerve root pain. Manipulation may be equally effective in dealing with recurrent attacks.

There is more limited evidence for the effectiveness of manipulation in patients with chronic low back pain. There is limited evidence available on the use of manipulation in patients with nerve root pain. Manipulation should not be used in patients with severe or progressive neurological deficit in view of the rare but serious risk of neurological complication. Serious neurological conditions should always be excluded before considering manipulation.

Rest versus active exercise

Avoid bed rest

There is strong evidence against the use of bed rest for more than one to three days for acute back pain. Bed rest may be used for up to one to two weeks for nerve root pain but there is no evidence to support its use for longer periods. In general, bed rest may be better regarded as a potentially harmful and undesirable consequence of back pain rather than a treatment. Prolonged or repeated bed rest should be avoided. There is no evidence for bed rest in hospital rather than at home.

Promote exercise

There is strong evidence for an active exercise and rehabilitation approach to back pain. The particular type of exercise may be less important. This is largely based on extensive evidence in chronic low back pain, but both theoretical principles and several controlled trials suggest that the earlier it is commenced the better – probably within the first two weeks and possibly within a few days for acute back pain. The same principles may apply to nerve root pain after the first one or two weeks.

Some temporary increase in pain is common at first, as occurs with most musculoskeletal conditions, but the patient should be reassured that hurt and harm are not the same and that such symptoms are normal at this stage. This is not a reason for reverting to passive management. There is no evidence that active exercise and early return to work increases the risk of recurrence. On the contrary, patients treated with active exercise and early return to work have fewer recurrences, less additional time off work and less health care over the following two years.

Aerobic, endurance exercises such as walking, cycling and swimming are effective to improve physical fitness and modify pain mechanisms. They also produce minimal mechanical stress to the back and are most easily tolerated by most patients during the first two weeks. Strengthening exercises for abdominal and back muscles may be gradually increased, particularly after the first two weeks. There is little evidence to support any specific type of back exercise. The exercise programme must be active and must promote the patient's own physical activity and responsibility. Exercises should start from a tolerable level and then be increased by planned increments, rather than depending on reports of pain.

Biopychosocial assessment at six weeks

If managed properly, most patients with simple backache should have recovered sufficiently to return to work before six weeks, even if with some residual or recurrent symptoms. Those patients who have not returned to work by six weeks should be reassessed more thoroughly to find out why. The initial diagnostic triage should be re-checked.

There is also clear evidence that chronic disability due to simple backache is often associated with psychological and social factors. These commonly develop as a secondary consequence of continued pain and failed treatment, but may then become even more important than the original physical problem (Figure 3). Psychosocial factors should be considered carefully in all patients who are still off work after six weeks. If the patient has any previous history of psychological or social problems, or if there are any psychosocial "red flags", psychosocial factors should be considered at an earlier stage. A simple psychosocial history should then be part of the initial clinical assessment.

Psychosocial assessment can be carried out by the family doctor or therapist and does not necessarily require referral to a psychologist. However, it is important that the family doctor and therapist should be aware of and consider these issues.

Figure 3 – A biopsychosocial model of low back disability

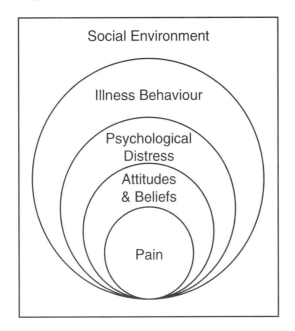

An overview of biopsychosocial assessment is set out below:

Bio:

- review diagnostic triage
  - nerve root problem
  - serious spinal pathology
- ESR and plain X-ray

Psycho:

- attitudes and beliefs about back pain
  - fear avoidance beliefs about activity and work
  - personal responsibility for pain and rehabilitation
- psychological distress and depressive symptoms
- illness behaviour

Social:

- family –
  - attitudes and beliefs about the problem
  - reinforcement of disability behaviour
- work
  - physical demands of job
  - job satisfaction
  - other health problems causing time off or job loss
  - non-health problems causing time off or job loss

Risk factors for chronicity

The risk factors for chronicity are set out below:

Previous history of low back pain
Total work loss (due to low back pain) in past twelve months
Radiating leg pain
Reduced straight leg raising
Signs of nerve root involvement
Reduced trunk muscle strength and endurance
Poor physical fitness
Self-rated health poor
Heavy smoking
Psychological distress and depressive symptoms
Disproportionate illness behaviour
Low job satisfaction
Personal problems – alcohol, marital, financial
Adversarial medico-legal proceedings

Low educational attainment and heavy physical occupation slightly increase the risk of low back pain and chronicity but markedly increase the difficulty of rehabilitation and retraining.

Multidisciplinary rehabilitation programme

The risk factors for chronicity show that as pain and disability become chronic, biopsychosocial factors become increasingly important. For this reason, purely physical treatment for chronic pain based on the disease model has a low success rate.

Traditional medical treatment not enough
Traditional medical treatment has certainly not solved our present epidermic of low back disability. Chronic pain and disability is a complex biopsychosocial problem which is perhaps better regarded as "activity intolerance". The main strategy should now be to "de-medicalise" symptoms and to regard the problem as one of rehabilitation.

Importance of a multidisciplinary approach
Clinical management should place equal emphasis on both the physical and psychosocial aspects of chronic pain and disability. A number of common elements can be identified from successful trials in chronic back pain. These are:
- Incremental exercise and fitness programme of physical reconditioning
- Behavioural medicine principles with functional objectives.
- Close liaison with the work place.

Varying levels of treatment
These principles can be implemented at several levels of intensity. Many of the principles have been achieved by a sole, part-time physical therapist working at the acute stage in a small work place. All of

the principles have been achieved effectively by a small research team consisting of a rehabilitation physician, a physical therapist and a psychologist working at the sub-acute stage in an occupational setting. In the case of chronic back cripples, comprehensive pain management programmes may require a large multidisciplinary team of medical and health care specialists. But these principles should form the basis of management of back pain by every family doctor, physiotherapist, osteopath, chiropractor or occupational health service.

Additional options for symptomatic relief

A large number of therapeutic options may be considered to provide symptomatic relief. However, there is no good scientific evidence that these options produce lasting benefits or that they change the natural history of back pain or sciatica. They should not be regarded as treatments in themselves but rather as symptomatic measures – the focus should be on active exercise and rehabilitation.

Therapeutic options for symptomatic relief are only valuable to the extent that they facilitate active exercise and rehabilitation. If symptoms and disability are not improved within six weeks, alternative or additional symptomatic and rehabilitative measures should be considered.

Additional therapeutic options for symptomatic relief include:

Drugs:
  analgesics
  NSAIDS
  muscle relaxants
  anti-depressants in low doses

Injections:
  trigger point injections
  epidural injections
  sclerosant injections
  facet injections

Physical modalities:
  heat/cold
  SWD and other electrotherapies
  TENS
  acupuncture
  biofeedback
  lumbosacral support
  sitting lumbar support
  shock relieving shoe insoles

Symptomatic measures to avoid

The treatments listed below should not be used. There is no evidence that they are of any benefit in low back pain or sciatica. They are also associated with harmful effects or risks which outweigh any potential benefit. In every case simpler and safer alternatives exist.

Do not use these treatments:

> Bed rest with traction
> Narcotics for more than two weeks
> Benzodiazepines (Diazepam) for more than two weeks
> Systemic steroids
> Colchicine
> Manipulation under general anaesthesia
> Plaster jacket

Secondary referral

If the patient with simple backache has not returned to work within three months, then primary care management has failed. Chronic pain and disability are then likely. If the patient has not returned to work within three months, if symptoms are not controlled, or if the patient has frequent recurrent attacks, then secondary referral should be considered. The aims of any secondary referral should be clearly identified and specified in the referral request.

The aims of the secondary referral may include:
- Second opinion for investigation, diagnosis, advice on management and reassurance
- Rehabilitation
- Vocational assessment and guidance
- Surgery
- Pain management

Final outcome measure: maintain productive activity; reduce work loss

The primary aim of management is to control pain and prevent disability: the result is to return the patient to normal function. The measure of successful management is the extent to which these are achieved.

Control of pain and prevention of disability go together. In the short term, relief of pain and distress and satisfaction with care may seem more important to the patient. Nevertheless, in the long term chronic disability is just as important and damaging as chronic pain. Moreover, return to normal function and to work are associated with reduced pain, while chronic pain and unemployment in themselves lead to psychosocial dysfunction. In the final outcome, the extent to which the patient returns to normal function is the best measure of control of pain.

Low back disability affects patients in many ways: restriction in activities of daily living, loss of productive activities and work loss. All are important, and management should set goals appropriate to the individual patient. In the previously disabled, the young, the elderly, housewives and the unemployed the aim may be to return to their formal function and to productive activities. In the previously disabled and in chronic pain patients realistic goals may fall short of that ideal. But for the working patient, loss of time from work with all its financial, psychological and social ill-effects on the individual and the family is the most important consequence of back pain. For the community, work loss is the most important measure of the social impact of back pain on employers, productivity, the economy and social costs. Success in halting the present epidemic of low back disability depends on reducing work loss. For all these reasons, how soon the patient returns to work and then remains at work is the single most important measure of low back disability. It is also the easiest and most objective to measure.

Work loss and return to work are also highly dependent upon work-related and socio-economic factors outwith medical control. Despite this, medical management of back pain can never be judged successful unless it reduces work loss.

What matters to the patient with backache is both control of pain and returning to normal function. The single most important measure of achieving this is work loss.

DIAGNOSTIC TRIAGE

of a patient presenting with low back pain with or without sciatic

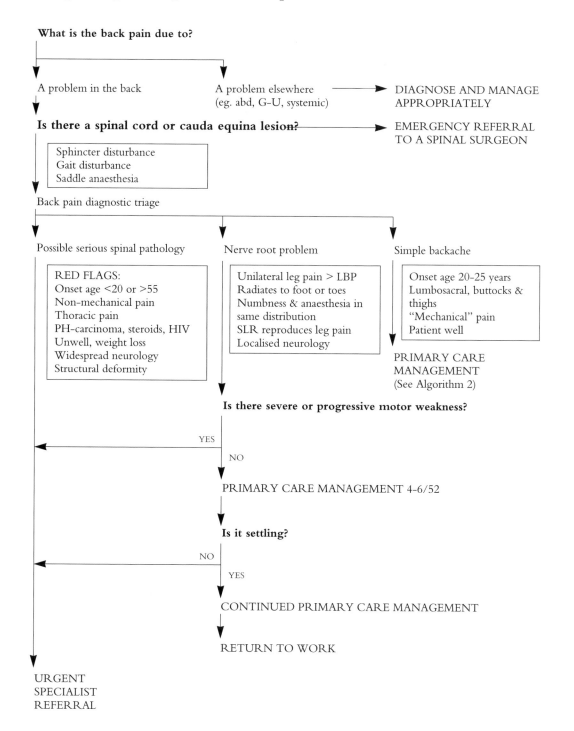

What is the back pain due to?

A problem in the back

A problem elsewhere
(eg. abd, G–U, systemic) → DIAGNOSE AND MANAGE APPROPRIATELY

Is there a spinal cord or cauda equina lesion? → EMERGENCY REFERRAL TO A SPINAL SURGEON

Sphincter disturbance
Gait disturbance
Saddle anaesthesia

Back pain diagnostic triage

Possible serious spinal pathology

RED FLAGS:
Onset age <20 or >55
Non-mechanical pain
Thoracic pain
PH-carcinoma, steroids, HIV
Unwell, weight loss
Widespread neurology
Structural deformity

Nerve root problem

Unilateral leg pain > LBP
Radiates to foot or toes
Numbness & anaesthesia in
same distribution
SLR reproduces leg pain
Localised neurology

Simple backache

Onset age 20-25 years
Lumbosacral, buttocks &
thighs
"Mechanical" pain
Patient well

PRIMARY CARE
MANAGEMENT
(See Algorithm 2)

Is there severe or progressive motor weakness?

YES

NO

PRIMARY CARE MANAGEMENT 4-6/52

Is it settling?

NO

YES

CONTINUED PRIMARY CARE MANAGEMENT

RETURN TO WORK

URGENT
SPECIALIST
REFERRAL

PRIMARY CARE MANAGEMENT OF SIMPLE BACKACHE

Is the patient acutely distressed?

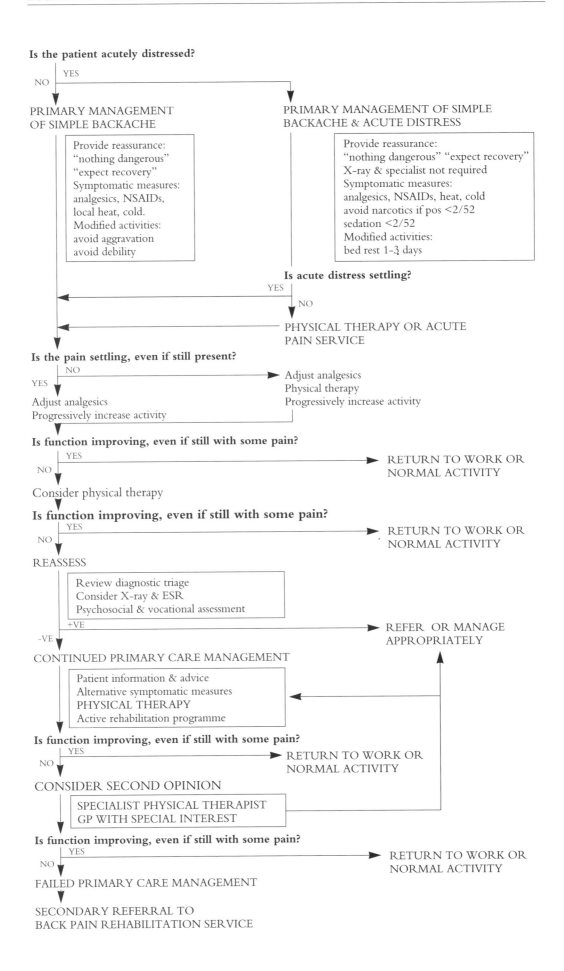

PRIMARY MANAGEMENT
OF SIMPLE BACKACHE

Provide reassurance:
"nothing dangerous"
"expect recovery"
Symptomatic measures:
analgesics, NSAIDs,
local heat, cold.
Modified activities:
avoid aggravation
avoid debility

PRIMARY MANAGEMENT OF SIMPLE
BACKACHE & ACUTE DISTRESS

Provide reassurance:
"nothing dangerous" "expect recovery"
X-ray & specialist not required
Symptomatic measures:
analgesics, NSAIDs, heat, cold
avoid narcotics if pos <2/52
sedation <2/52
Modified activities:
bed rest 1-3 days

Is acute distress settling?

YES   NO

PHYSICAL THERAPY OR ACUTE
PAIN SERVICE

Is the pain settling, even if still present?

NO

YES

Adjust analgesics
Progressively increase activity

Adjust analgesics
Physical therapy
Progressively increase activity

Is function improving, even if still with some pain?

YES

NO

RETURN TO WORK OR
NORMAL ACTIVITY

Consider physical therapy

Is function improving, even if still with some pain?

YES

NO

RETURN TO WORK OR
NORMAL ACTIVITY

REASSESS

Review diagnostic triage
Consider X-ray & ESR
Psychosocial & vocational assessment

+VE

-VE

REFER OR MANAGE
APPROPRIATELY

CONTINUED PRIMARY CARE MANAGEMENT

Patient information & advice
Alternative symptomatic measures
PHYSICAL THERAPY
Active rehabilitation programme

Is function improving, even if still with some pain?

YES

NO

RETURN TO WORK OR
NORMAL ACTIVITY

CONSIDER SECOND OPINION

SPECIALIST PHYSICAL THERAPIST
GP WITH SPECIAL INTEREST

Is function improving, even if still with some pain?

YES

NO

RETURN TO WORK OR
NORMAL ACTIVITY

FAILED PRIMARY CARE MANAGEMENT

SECONDARY REFERRAL TO
BACK PAIN REHABILITATION SERVICE

Membership of sounding board on management guidelines

Invited Organisations

Anglo European College of Chiropractic
Parkwood Road
Bournemouth
Dorset BH5 2DF

Association of British Neurological Surgeons
c/o Mr T A J Hide
Dunardie
Kilbarchan Road
Bridge of Weir
Renfrewshire

Back Pain Society
PO Box 342
Harrow
Middlesex HA3 9BA

British Chiropractic Association
29 Whitley Street
Reading
Berks RG2 0EG

British Institute of Musculoskeletal Medicine
27 Green Lane
Northwood
Middlesex HA6 2PX

British Orthopaedic Association
35 Lincoln's Inn Fields
London WC2

British School of Osteopathy
1-4 Suffolk Street
London SW1Y 4HG

British Society of Rheumatology
3 St Andrew's Place
London NW1

Chartered Society of Physiotherapy
14 Bedford Row
London WC1R 4ED

College of Occupational Therapists
6-8 Marshalsea Road
London SE1 1HL

College of Osteopaths
1 Furze Hill Road
Borehamwood
Herts

Faculty of Occupational Medicine
c/o Royal College of Physicians
11 St Andrew's Place
London NW1

General Council and Register of Osteopaths
56 London Street
Reading
Berks RG1 4SQ

National Back Pain Association
31-33 Park Road
Teddington
Middlesex TW11 0AB

Osteopathic Association
206 Chesterton Road
Cambridge CB4 1NE

Pain Society
c/o Dr Diamond
Frenchay Hospital
Bristol BS16 1LE

Primary Care Rheumatology Society
85 South Parade
Northallerton
North Yorkshire DLT 8SL
Royal College of General Practitioners
14 Princes Gate
Hyde Park
London SW7 1PU

Primary Care Rheumatology Society
85 South Parade
Northallerton
North Yorkshire DLT 8SL

Royal College of General Practitioners
14 Princes Gate
Hyde Park
London SW7 1PU

Royal College of Nursing
20 Cavendish Square
London W1M 0AB

Royal College of Physicians
11 St Andrew's Place
London NW1

Royal College of Surgeons
Lincoln's Inn Fields
London WC2

Society for Back Pain Research
30 Queens Street
Huddersfield
Yorks HD1 2SP

Society of Teachers of the Alexander Technique
10 London House
Fulham Road
London SW10

Delegates and Contributors

Guest speaker:
Dr S Bigos
Chairman, US Management Guidelines Panel
SEATTLE USA

Dr C Ballard
Society of Teachers of Alexander Technique
London

Dr M Bryn-Jones
National Back Pain Association
Middlesex

Dr P Buckle
University of Surrey

Dr K Burton
Director of Spinal Research Unit
Huddersfield University

Mrs N Cogan
Physiotherapy Officer
Department of Health

Mr M Cummins
PMD ASPU
Department of Health
Dr J R Jenner
Clinical Director/Consultant Rheumatologist
Addenbrookes Hospital

Mr P Davis
Society of Orthopaedic Nursing
London

Mrs P Edwards
NUR
Department of Health

Mr S Fielding
Council of Osteopaths
Kent

Mrs M Fry
HEF(A)4
Department of Health

Mr J Goodman
College of Osteopaths
Herts

Ms M Hodgson
Senior Occupational Therapist
Atkinson Morley Hospital
London

Mr I Hutchison
President
British Chiropractic Association
Essex

DR J R Jenner
Clinical Director
Consultant Rheumatolgist
Addenbrookes Hospital

Dr D Justins
Department of Anaesthetics
St Thomas Hospital

Dr P Leech
HCD - SD
Department of Health

Dr E B MacDonald
Department of Public Health
University of Glasgow

Dr C J Main
Clinical Psychologist
Salford

Dr J Matthews
Department of Rheumatology
St Thomas Hospital

Prof T Meade
Medical Research Council
London

Dr R Million
Rheumatic Disease Centre
Salford

Mr M Morrison
Consultant Orthopaedic Surgeon
Wiltshire

Prof R W Porter
Consultant Orthopaedic Surgeon
Aberdeen

Dr Randell
British School of Osteopathy
London

Dr K Rogers
Pain Relief Centre
Glasgow

Mrs. S Richards
Occupational Therapy Officer
Department of Health

Dr D Rothman
HC(M)1
Department of Health

Mr G J Sharp
General Council & Register of Osteopaths
Berkshire

Mr J A N Shepperd
Consultant Orthopaedic Surgeon
East Sussex

Mr C Standen
British School of Osteopathy
London

Dr D Stubbs
University of Surrey

Dr J Wedley
Kingston upon Thames

Mr P Wells
Physiotherapy Centre
London

Appendix D Literature references for management guidelines

DSS Statistics (Figure 1 of Management Guidelines) From DSS Analytical Services Division 1B (Epidemiological Review Annex)

Probability of return to work -v- time off work (Figure 2 of Management Guidelines) From Epidemiological Review Annex

International Association for the Study of Pain, Task Force on Pain in the Workplace, Draft outline of management for acute low back pain (1993)

US Agency of Health Care Policy and Research, (AHCPR) Management Guidelines Panel, outline of acute management Algorithm of diagnostic triage. Brit J Hosp Med 1982, 28: 87-219

Waddell G, Hamblen D L, The differential diagnosis of back pain. Practitioner 1983, 227: 1167-1175

Deyo R A, Rainville J, Kent D L, What can the history and physical examination tell us about low back pain? J Amer Med Assoc 1992, 268: 760-765

Royal College of Radiologists, Making the best use of a department of radiology: guidelines for doctors, 1989

Editorial, Guidelines for radiological investigation. Brit Med J 1991, 303: 797-798

Royal College of Radiologists Working Party, A multicentre audit of hospital referral for radiological investigation in England and Wales. Brit Med J 1991, 303: 809-812

Halpin S F S, Yeoman L, Dundas D D, Radiographic examination of the lumbar spine in a community: an audit of current practice. Brit Med J 1991, 303:813-815

Biopsychosocial model (Figure 3 of Management Guidelines) from Clin Rheumatol 1992, 6: 523-557

Waddell G, Turk D C, Clinical assessment of low back pain. In Turk D C, Melzack R (Eds) Handbook of pain assessment. 1992, New York: Guildford Press

Lloyd D C E F, Troup J D G, Recurrent back pain and its prediction. J Soc Occup Med 1983, 33:66-74

Biering-Sorensen F, Physical measurements as risk indicators for low-back trouble over a one-year period. Spine 1984, 9:106-119

Burton A K, Tillotson K M, Prediction of the clinical course of low-back trouble using multi-variable models. Spine 1991, 16:7-14

Biering-Sorensen F, Thomsen C, Medical, social and occupational history as risk indicators for low-back trouble in a general population. Spine 1986, 11:720-725

Deyo R A, Diehl A K, Psychosocial predictors of disability in patients with low back pain. J Rheumatol, 1988 15: 1557-1564

Summary of scientific evidence on treatment for acute low back pain. Based on draft review of controlled trials by US Management Guidelines Panel (1992)

Explanation of Evidence Tables on controlled trials of treatment. US Management Guidelines Panel (AHCPR)

Evidence Table on controlled trials of bed rest (AHCPR)

Deyo R A, Diehl A K, Rosenthal M, How many days of bed rest for acute low back pain? A randomised clinical trial. New England J Med 1986, 315: 1064-1070

Gilbert J R, et al, Clinical trial of common treatments for low back pain in family practice. Brit Med J 1985. 291:791-794

Szpalski M, Hayez J P, How many days of bed rest for acute low back pain? Objective assessment of trunk function. Eur Spine J 1992, 1:29-31

Waddell G, Biopsychosocial analysis of low back pain. Clin Rheumatol 1992, 6:523-557

Lindstrom I, et al, Mobility, strength, and fitness after a graded activity program for patients with subacute low back pain. Spine 1992, 17:641-652

Evidence Table on controlled trials of flexion, extension, passive extension (McKenzie), and strengthening exercises (AHCPR)

Koes B W, et al, Physiotherapy exercises and back pain: a blinded review. Brit Med J 1991, 302:1572-1576

Sims-Williams H, Jayson M, et al, Controlled trials of mobilisation and manipulation for patients with low back pain in general practice. Brit Med J 1978, 2:1338-1340

Sims-Williams H, Jayson M, et al, Controlled trial of mobilisation and manipulation for low back pain: hospital patients. Brit Med J 1979, 2:1318-1320

Kane R L, et al, Manipulating the patient: A comparison of the effectiveness of physician and chiropractor care. Lancet 1974, 1333-1336

Meade T W, et al, Low back pain of mechanical origin: randomised comparison of chiropractic and hospital outpatient treatment. Brit Med J 1990, 300:1431-1437

Koes B W, et al, Randomised clinical trial of manipulative therapy and physiotherapy for persistent back and neck complaints: results of one year follow up. Brit Med J 1992, 304:601-605

Koes B W, et al, The effectiveness of manual therapy, physiotherapy and treatment by the general practitioner for nonspecific back and neck complaints: a randomised clinical trial. Spine 1992, 17:28-35

Evidence Table of controlled trials of manipulation (AHCPR)

Shekelle, P G et al, Spinal manipulation for low-back pain. Ann Int Med 1992, 117:590-598

Bronfort G, Effectiveness of spinal manipulation and adjustments. In Haldeman S(Ed) Principles and Practice of Chiropractic. Second Edition 1992. Norwalk: Appleton & Lange

AHCPR bibliography for Evidence Tables.

Organisations that Submitted Papers To The Sounding Board Conference.

Anglo-European College of Chiropractic

British Chiropractic Association

British Institute of Musculo-Skeletal Medicine

British Orthopaedic Association

British School of Osteopathy

Chartered Society of Physiotherapists

College of Osteopaths

General Council and Register of Osteopaths

National Back Pain Association

Pain Society

Society of Teachers of the Alexander Technique

Spinal Research Unit: University of Huddersfield

Royal College of General Practitioners

Royal College of Physicians

Additional Material Submitted by Members of the Sounding Board

Bigos J S, Andary T, The practitioner's guide to the industrial back problem: Part I. Helping the patient with the symptom and pathology. Seminars in Spine Surgery 1992, 4:42-54

Waddell G 1993 Simple low back pain: rest or active exercise? Ann Rheum Dis 52:317-319.

Jette A M et al 1994 Physical therapy episodes of care for patients with low back pain. Phys Ther 74:101-110

Di Fabio R P, Efficacy of manual therapy. In Rothstein J M (Ed) Manual Therapy. An American Physical Therapy Association Monograph: Alexandria VA 1992

Anderson R, et al, A meta-analysis of clinical trials of spinal manipulation. J Manip Physiol Ther 1992, 15:181-194

Linton J J, et al controlled study of the effects of an early intervention on acute musculoskeletal pain problems. Pain 1993, 54:353-359

Cherkin D C, Deyo R A, Nonsurgical hospitalization for low-back pain: Is it necessary?. Spine 1993, 18:1728-1735

Frank A, Low back pain. Brit Med J 1993, 306:901-909

Edwards B C, et al, A Physical approach to the rehabilitation of patients disabled by chronic low back pain. Med J Austral 1992, 156:167-172

Ponte D J, et al, A preliminary report on the use of the McKenzie protocol versus Williams protocol in the treatment of low back pain. J Orthop Sports Phys Ther 1984, 6:130-139

Moffett J A K, et al, A controlled prospective study to evaluate the effectiveness of a back school in the relief of chronic low back pain. Spine 1986, 11:120-122

Hackett G I, et al, Management of joint and soft tissue injuries in three general practices: value of on-site physiotherapy. Brit J Gen Pract 1993, 43:61-64

Lew P, et al, British Medical Journal article 300:1431-1437: Low back pain of mechanical origin: randomised comparison of chiropractic and hospital outpatient treatment - an MPAA critical evaluation

Fairbank J C T, et al, The Oswestry low back pain disability questionnaire. Physiotherapy 1980, 66:271-273

Lamb F, Frost H, Exercises - the other root of our profession. Physiotherapy 1993, 79:772

Saunders L, Chiropractic: Coping with costs. Physiotherapy 1993, 79:264.

Sharp G J, Low back pain: the osteopathic approach. Based on an investigation and analysis of competencies required for osteopathic practice (CROP). Unpublished manuscript

Pringle M, Tyreman S, Study of 500 patients attending an osteopathic practice. Brit J Gen Pract 1993, 43:15-18

Szemlskyj A O, The difference between holistic osteopathic practice and manipulation. Holistic Med 1990, 5:67-79

Haldeman S, Rubinstein S M, 1992 Cauda equina syndrome in patients undergoing manipulation of the lumbar spine. Spine 17:1469-1473

Mathews J A, et al, Back pain and sciatica: controlled trials of manipulation, traction, sclerosant and epidural injections. Brit J. Rheumatol 1987, 26:416-423

Occupational Therapy and back pain. Unpublished manuscript

Mathews J A, Management of back pain and sciatica. Unpublished manuscript

MacDonald E, Low back pain: The role of the Faculty of Occupational Medicine

Blow R J, Jayson M I V, Back pain. In Edwards S W, McCallen R J, Taylor P J (Eds), Fitness for work. Royal College of Physicians & Faculty of Occupational Medicine 1988 pp 142-161

Buckle P, Stubbs D, The contribution of ergonomics to the rehabilitation of back pain patients. J Soc Occup Med 1989, 39:56-60

Morrison M C T, Guidelines for the management of back pain and/or leg pain. Unpublished manuscript

Shepperd J A N, et al, Percutaneous disc surgery. Clin Orthop & Rel Res 1989, 238:43-49

Shepperd J, The role of the surgeon in diagnosis and management of low back disorders. Unpublished manuscript

Shepperd J A N, Wilson J, Spinal probing: its role in prevention of pitfalls and complications in minimal surgery. Unpublished manuscript

Wedley J R, Spinal cord stimulation. Unpublished manuscript

Rogers K M, Pain control. Unpublished manuscript

Jarvis K B, et al, Cost per case comparison of back injury claims of chiropractic versus medical management for conditions with identical diagnostic codes. J Occ Med 1991, 33:847-852

Breen A C, Communicating with 'medics' in the United Kingdom. Eur J Chiropractic 1982, 30:65-69

Breen A C, Chiropractic: the case for its availability in the National Health Service. Health Development Review (Complementary Therapies) Aberdeen 1993

British Chiropractic Association: Code of ethics

Manga P, et al, The effectiveness and cost-effectiveness of chiropractic management of low-back pain. Ontario Ministry of Health 1993

Haldeman S, et al, Guidelines for Chiropractic quality assurance and practice parameters: Proceedings of the Mercy Center Consensus Conference (US) 1993

Coulter A et al, Outcome of general practitioner referrals to specialist outpatient clinics for back pain. Brit J Gen Prac 1991, 41:450-453

Roland M, Dixon M 1989 The role of an educational booklet in managing patients presenting with back pain in primary care. In Roland M Jenner J (Eds) Back pain: new approaches to education and rehabilitation, Manchester Univ

CSAG back pain committee visits to districts visit questionnaire

1.   In your District what are the number of the following:

persons in the population

| |

whole time equivalent NHS clinical staff

general practitioners (fundholding)

| |

general practitioners (non fundholding)

| |

physiotherapists working in the NHS

| |

orthopaedic consultants

| |

rheumatology consultants

| |

radiologists

| |

district general hospitals

| |

community hospitals

| |

NHS Trusts

| |

directly managed units

| |

complementary medicine practices

osteopathy

| |

chiropractic

| |

clinics

pain clinics per month

| |

direct access physiotherapy clinics per month

| |

2.   Looking at the draft Management Guidelines for back pain, what is the position in your District on the following:

	Satisfactory	Unsatisfactory
emergency referral to a neurosurgeon within a matter of hours	☐	☐
urgent referral within two weeks	☐	☐
access to a therapist within three weeks	☐	☐
psychosocial assessment at six weeks	☐	☐
multidisciplinary rehabilitation programme	☐	☐
very selective referral for x-ray	☐	☐

	Yes	No
3 Are there examples of back pain clinical guidelines?	☐	☐
and/or back pain patient leaflets	☐	☐

If yes, please enclose

| 4. Are there specific examples of training in back pain management in clinical training in the District? | ☐ | ☐ |

If yes, please give details:

Please return this questionnaire with supporting information to:

Appendix F | Organisations and post-graduate training in musculo-skeletal medicine and manipulation

A. Physiotherapists

The following organisations are members of the British Association of Chartered Physiotherapists in Manipulation (BACPIM), and provide post-registration education and training in the management of neuromusculoskeletal disorders.

Manipulative Association of Chartered Physiotherapists
c/o Mrs J McClusky
Windle Cottage
Plough Lane
Ormskirk
Lancs L40 6JL

Society of Orthopaedic Medicine
c/o Monica Kesson
Faversham Physiotherapy Clinic
The Mall
Faversham
Kent ME13 8JL

MSc Physiotherapy (University College)
c/o Ann Thomson
Middlesex School of Physiotherapy
Arthur Stanley House
London

Orthopaedic Medicine International
c/o E Kelly
55 Percival Road
Enfield
Middlesex EN1 1CS

McKenzie Institute
c/o Malcolm Robinson
92 Lindridge Road
Sutton Coldfield
West Midlands B75 6HJ

Sheffield Combined Manipulation Course
c/o John Cleak
School of Health Studies
Sheffield Hallam University
Sheffield.

B. Medical Practitioners

1. British Institute of Musculoskeletal Medicine
Hon Sec: Dr P Skew
27 Green Lane
Northwood
Middlesex HA6 2PX

3 course modules in musculoskeletal medicine each year in association with Southampton University.

2. Society of Orthopaedic Medicine
Joint organisation of doctors and physiotherapists (address as above)
4 day courses throughout UK each year.

These two organisations, jointly with the American Association of Orthopaedic Medicine, issue the Journal of Orthopaedic Medicine.

c/o Dr R M Ellis, Chief Editor
Department of Rheumatology
District General Hospital
Salisbury SP2 8BJ

3. Society of Apothecaries of London
Apothecaries Hall
Black Friars Lane
London EC4 6EJ

Diploma in musculoskeletal medicine.

4. British School of Osteopathy
1-4 Suffolk Street
London SW1Y 4HG

Short course for doctors. Fulltime course depending on prior clinical experience. Examination for Doctor of Osteopathy and eligibility for membership of Register of Osteopaths (MRO).

5. London College of Osteopathic Medicine
8-10 Boston Place
London NW1 6QH

Courses and examination in osteopathic medicine leading to Doctor of Osteopathy, membership of the College and eligibility for membership of Register of Osteopaths (MRO).

6. Primary Care Rheumatology Society

Journal: Musculoskeletal Medicine

55 South Parade
Northallerton
North Yorkshire DL7 8BY

Note: This list is for information only and may be incomplete. These organisations do not necessarily have any official status or national recognition.

 Appendix G | Economic modelling of the effects of the management guidelines and service recommendations on NHS resource use

Introduction

The aim of this analysis is to estimate the annual cost to the NHS of implementing the management guidelines and service recommendations.

It is important to consider the resource and cost implications of our proposals, though we recognise the weaknesses and limitations of any such analysis. We start from the best available figures of current NHS use and costs (Annex), though we have already noted the possible errors of these estimates. There are many assumptions to such a model which we have made to the best of our ability, and we believe that they are reasonable and conservative. Moreover, the assumptions are explicit and the model permits alternative assumptions to be tested.

We analyse the possible impact of the guidelines and recommendations if they were fully implemented. Many of the recommendations are for changes in NHS services to enable the management guidelines to be put into practice. Conversely, however, other proposed changes in services depend on clinical management changing in line with the guidelines. The recommendations and management guidelines are clearly linked, and so are the cost implications. Obviously, the major question and assumption in any such model is the extent to which the proposals are implemented (Goldman 1990), so two more realistic scenarios are then considered. The minimum effect is assumed to be where the guidelines and recommendations are 25% implemented or put into practice by 25% of physicians and therapists. The maximum effect is assumed to be where the guidelines and recommendations are 75% implemented or put into practice by 75% of physicians and therapists.

Determining the Effects of the Management Guidelines on Resource Use

The management guidelines were based as far as possible on controlled trials. These same trials provide an estimate of the potential improvement which could be achieved by improved management. Table 1 lists various clinical outcomes from these trials showing percentage improvement compared with the control groups. The references are shown in brackets.

79

Table 1 - Potential clinical benefit of improved management for simple backache based on controlled trials.

Outcome measure	Acute	Sub-acute	Chronic
Pain	35%	50%	20-55%
	(2)	(12)	(4,9,15)
Activities of daily living	10-40%	20-50%	10-25%
	(2,3,6)	(5,12)	(4,9,15)
Duration of work loss	40-45%		30%
	(2,3)		(18)
Work loss over one year		30-75%	
		(14,22,23)	
Chronically disabled		75-80%	30-50%
		(13,14)	(10,16,21)
Health care use		35%	30-50%
		(5)	(4,16)

If these guidelines were fully implemented and if they achieved the same level of success as in published trials, then potentially clinical outcomes could be improved by the order of 30-50%. At present this has been demonstrated in a trial situation with selected groups of patients, research resources and carefully controlled conditions. The effects are likely to be less in routine clinical practice. Few of these trials are in Britain though, in principle, it should be possible to achieve comparable clinical outcomes here.

Effects of management guidelines

The management guidelines include four main changes in clinical practice: a reduction in the number of x-rays, altered analgesic use, increased use of manipulation and active rehabilitation.

If the Royal College of Radiologists guidelines were followed, then an estimated 50 % of x-rays for back pain could be avoided (RCR 1993, Halpin et al 1991). Under our assumptions the effect of minimum implementation would be a 12.5% fall in the number of x-rays while the effect of maximum implementation would be a 37.5 % fall in the number of x-rays. In addition to the resource and cost effects, this could save many people from unnecessary irradiation and three to seven radiation deaths each year. Changing the number of x-rays is not likely to have any significant effect on use of other resources.

More rapid recovery and prevention of chronic disability should reduce the duration that analgesics are required. Based on the above trials this might reduce the cost of prescribed drugs by one third if it were fully implemented. It is uncertain how this might affect expenditure on over-the-counter medicine.

Manipulation and active rehabilitation are likely to have the greatest effect. In principle, the improved clinical outcomes are likely to reduce the following NHS resource use : GP consultations, x-rays, prescribed drugs, routine outpatient clinics, A & E attendances and non-surgical hospitalisation for simple backache. If clinical outcomes are improved by 30-50%, we have assumed conservatively that this could result in reduced demand on services of the order of 30%. The minimum and maximum effects in practice are therefore of the order of 7.5% and 22.5%.

If all GPs implemented the guidelines, there could be a 30 % reduction in repeat GP consultations for back pain. Fewer repeat consultations would again reduce the number of repeat prescriptions.

Similarly, fully implementing these changes in management could reduce the number of routine out-patient consultations, A & E attendances and in-patient bed-days for simple backache by 30%. Allowing for the proportion of these resources used for nerve root problems and serious spinal pathology, full implementation of the Management Guidelines might reduce routine outpatient consultations and A & E attendances by 25%, and in-patient bed-days by 15%. There are, however, specific service recommendations on the use of out-patient clinics, A & E and in-patient care for simple backache which might have much greater effects than the management guideline alone (see later). There might be some reduction in private consultations and private physical therapy but this is impossible to estimate.

Table 2 summarises the potential minimum and maximum effects on resource use of implementing the Management Guidelines.

Table 2 – Estimates of the possible effects of the Management Guidelines

NHS Resource use	Minimum effects	Maximum effects
GP consultations	7.5 % reduction in repeat consultations	22.5 % reduction in repeat consultations
X-rays	12.5% reduction	37.5% reduction
Prescribed drugs	8% reduction	25% reduction
Physical therapy	Reorganisation of NHS physical therapy	

Resource Consequences of the Service Recommendations

We have already considered the likely effects of the management guidelines in terms of changed clinical practice and improved clinical outcomes. However, the recommendations on services will have a direct and much greater effect on costs and savings over and above the effects of improved clinical practice from the management guidelines.

The main changes in services to be considered are:
- physical therapy.
- a Back Pain Rehabilitation Service
- reduction in routine outpatient consultations
- an acute pain service
- reduction in non-surgical hospitalisation

At present, one million patients receive NHS physical therapy for back pain. Each receives an average of seven treatment sessions, totalling seven million NHS physical therapy sessions. At present, very few patients receive NHS physical therapy for acute pain within the first six weeks, and the majority are treated for chronic pain. If the management guidelines were fully put into practice it is estimated that 1 million patients would be referred at the acute stage for physical therapy (District Visits). At the acute stage, however, there is a high natural resolution rate and treatment is more successful. Together with the improved clinical outcomes produced by increased availability of manipulation and active rehabilitation, the average number of physical therapy sessions required for these acute patients should be reduced to four (District Visits). This would give a total of four million acute physical therapy sessions. Under our assumptions of minimum and maximum implementation, there would be between one million (minimum implementation) and three million (maximum implementation) acute physical therapy sessions for back pain.

Physical therapy will also play a major role in the Back Pain Rehabilitation Service. An additional six million physical therapy sessions for more chronic back pain are allowed for this, which will be included in the estimates for the Back Pain Rehabilitation Service (see below). Again assuming minimum and maximum implementation, this would require a minimum of 1.5 and maximum of 4.5

million physical therapy sessions.

Table 3 – Estimated changes in use of NHS physical therapy

	Current practice	Minimum implementation	Maximum implementation
Current practice	7.0	5.25	1.75
Direct referrals for acute back pain	minimal	1.0	3.0
Back Pain Rehabilitation Service	0	1.5	4.5
Total physical therapy sessions	7.0	7.75	9.25

It is proposed that secondary care for those patients with back pain who do not settle with management in primary care should be provided by a Back Pain Rehabilitation Service. Assuming the improvements generated in primary care by the management guidelines, it is estimated that 0.5 million patients would be referred to the Back Pain Rehabilitation Service. These are more selected patients who would already have failed management in primary care, so on average they are likely to require more treatment. We have therefore allowed an average of three out-patient medical consultations (compared with 1.5 at present) and twelve therapy sessions (compared with seven at present). The therapy includes physical, psychological and occupational therapy, some of which would be provided on a group basis, with staff savings. The costs of educational material are considered below. Medical consultation cost are taken to be the same as the current cost of an average outpatient visit, and the therapy sessions approximately the same as the current cost of NHS physiotherapy sessions. On this basis the estimated cost per patient is £200. Under our minimum and maximum assumptions the cost of a new Back Pain Rehabilitation Service would be £25 million and £75 million.

Ideally, the Back Pain Rehabilitation Service should provide secondary care for all patients with simple backache, who at present account for 90% of all routine outpatient clinic visits to the "back pain specialties". Under our minimum and maximum assumptions, this would reduce the number of outpatient attendances for back pain at routine clinics in these specialties from 2.4 million to between 1.9 million (minimum implementation) and 0.8 million (maximum implementation). The corresponding savings would be between £16 million and £49 million.

An acute pain service is recommended for patients with acute back pain which does not respond to standard management in primary care. This would be a specialist service either on an outpatient or a day case basis. It is estimated that there could be up to 0.5 million referrals to acute pain services (District Visits). Based on current outpatient practice (Annex), these patients might require an average of 1.5 consultations. We have also allowed an average of one minor procedure. (Any further physical therapy costs are costed separately above). As some of this will be emergency care, we have allowed an increased cost of an out-patient consultation as £40 and the cost of a minor day case procedure as £100. The cost per patient is thus £180 and the estimated total annual cost of the acute pain service would be £90 million if it was fully implemented. Under our minimum assumptions the cost of such a service would be £22 million and under our maximum assumptions £68 million.

The greatest potential gain of the acute pain service is to largely replace emergency admission for control of acute pain and distress, hence reducing non-surgical hospitalisation. Approximately 100,000 patients are admitted to hospital as in-patients for a total of 770,000 bed-days for treatment of low back disorders. 24,000 have a surgical operation and a further 33,000 have more minor procedures, some as day-cases. Surgical cases, those undergoing minor procedures and the small number admitted for investigation and treatment of serious spinal pathology amount to approximately half the total bed-days for back disorders and these are not affected by our recommendations. However, half the total bed occupancy is non-surgical hospitalisation of simple backache. Under the recommendations for more appropriate management and services, very few admissions should be necessary for simple backache. Total bed occupancy for all back disorders could therefore be almost halved. Under our minimum assumptions the cost saving would be £13 million and under our maximum assumption would be £38 million.

The acute pain service and the effects of the management guidelines should ideally largely replace A & E visits. However, as patients may decide to go directly to A & E without consulting and hence being influenced by their GP we have assumed conservatively that the number will only be halved. Allowing for either a 25% or a 75% implementation, the number of A & E attendances would be reduced from 480,000 to either 420,000 or 300,000 at a cost saving of between £2.1 million and £6.3 million. An acute pain service should ideally stop, or at least reduce the number of domiciliary visits by consultants. There is no central information on the current level of such services but this is unlikely to have much effect on the overall net cost of back pain services.

Improved clinical services in general, and a better acute pain service in particular, should reduce the demand on pain clinics for intractable chronic pain. There is, however, a considerable back-log of such cases. This effect is therefore difficult to quantify in the short term and has been omitted from the estimated savings.

It is recommended that educational material relating to the management guidelines should be produced and distributed. Distribution of approximately 50,000 copies of the management guidelines to all general practitioners and relevant clinical specialties is estimated to cost £0.25 million. Patient information material for three million patients each year is estimated to cost £3 million.

Table 4 estimates the additional costs and savings of the service recommendations.

Table 4 – Estimated additional costs and savings of the service recommendations (£millions)

	Minimum Assumptions	Maximum Assumptions
Back Pain Rehabilitation Service	25	75
Routine outpatient clinics	-16	-49
Acute pain service	18	54
A & E Attendances	-2	-6
Inpatient days	-13	-38
Educational material	1	3
Total	**+ £13**	**+ £39**

Combined Effects of the Management Guidelines and Service Recommendations

Table 5 estimates the combined effects on resource use of the service recommendations and management guidelines. Broadly, the service recommendations are cost-neutral. This is largely a question of re-deploying existing resources. Initially, modest developmental funding will be required to implement the changes. Ultimately, there could be slight cost savings.

Table 5 – Estimated health care costs allowing for the combined effects of the Management Guidelines and the Service Recommendations (£millions)

NHS Resource Use	Current costs	Minimum Assumption	Maximum Assumption
GP consultations	130	120	101
X rays	45	39	28
Prescribed drugs	48	44	37
Physical therapy ★	63	56	43
		(★ + 14)	(★ + 40)
Acute back pain services	0	22	68
Routine outpatient clinics	72	56	23
Back Pain Rehabilitation Service	0	25	75
A & E Attendances	17	15	11
Inpatient bed-days	106	93	68
Educational material	0	1	3
Total	481	471	457

★ Additional cost of physical therapy provided in and included in the costs of the Back Pain Rehabilitation Service

Total social costs

The major costs of back pain are in work loss and DSS benefits. Current estimates are £480 for annual NHS costs compared with £3.8 billion for lost production and £1.4 billion for DSS benefits (Annex). The above model is mainly about the effects of the management guidelines and service recommendations on NHS costs. The greatest potential savings, however, are in work loss and DSS benefits.

The likely effect of improved clinical management and improved NHS services for back pain on work loss and DSS claims is difficult to estimate. These depend to some extent on health care but also to a large extent on social, socio-economic and employment influences. Benefits paid also depend on DSS regulations and practice. Once patients are off work for more than twenty-eight weeks and particularly once they have lost their job, the chances of returning to work are low irrespective of health care (Epidemiology Review). Oland & Tveiten (1991) attempted to replicate the US trial of work hardening (Mayer et al 1987) in Finland. More than 80% of the US patients in the active rehabilitation programme returned to work but less than 25% of those in Finland managed to do so. In Finland return to work in the active rehabilitation group was not significantly better than in the control group. Oland & Tveiten concluded that the most important differences from the results in US were patient selection and the health and social security systems. Similar findings have been reported from Sweden by Aberg (1984). The health and social security systems in Britain appear to be much closer to Finland and Sweden than to US so the effects of these proposals on work loss are open to question.

Nevertheless, improved clinical management and improved NHS services for back pain should have some effect on work loss and DSS benefits. Every one per cent improvement would save £38 million in lost production and £14 million in DSS benefits. A modest 10% improvement would save £0.5 billion within one year. This is not over-optimistic: the impact of back pain has increased by this amount in the last year alone. Achieving a 10% improvement would simply restore the position to what it was a year ago. Conversely, even if we only managed to hold the current situation from deteriorating further, we would save an estimated £0.5 billion increase in the total cost of back pain to society next year.

Summary

It is impossible to be sure of the exact costs of implementing the service recommendations. Individual recommendations require additional resources and developmental funding, particularly physical therapy, a Back Pain Rehabilitation Service and acute pain services. There are also major savings, particularly in inappropriate and unproductive use of x-rays, routine specialty clinics and non-surgical hospitalisation of patients with simple backache. Overall, the service recommendations are cost-neutral and it is largely a question of re-deploying resources more effectively. The greatest potential saving to society, however, is in the much greater costs of work loss and DSS benefits. Every 1% improvement could save £38 million in lost production and £14 million in DSS benefits. If we do nothing to improve the situation, total social costs of back pain in Britain are likely to continue to increase by up to £0.5 billion per annum.

References

1. Aberg J 1984 Evaluation of an advanced back pain rehabilitation program. Spine 9:317-318.

2. Anderson R et al 1992 A meta-analysis of clinical trials of spinal manipulation. J Manip Physiol Ther 15:181-194.

3. Deyo RA et al 1986 How many days of bedrest for acute low back pain? New Eng J Med 315:1064-1070.

4. Deyo RA et al 1990 A controlled trial of transcutaneous electrical nerve stimulation (TENS) and exercise for chronic low back pain. N Eng J Med 322:1627-1634.

5. Fordyce WE et al 1986 Acute back pain: a control group comparison of behavioural -vs- traditional management methods. J Behav Med 9:127-140.

6. Gilbert JR et al 1985 Clinical trial of common treatments for low back pain in family practice. Brit Med J 291:791-794.

7. Goldman L 1990 Changing physician's behaviour (Editorial) N Eng J Med 322:1424-1525.

8. Halpin SFS et al 1991 Radiographic examination of the lumbar spine in a community: an audit of current practice. Brit Med J 303:813-815.

9. Harkapaa K et al 1989 A controlled study on the outcome of inpatient and outpatient treatment of low back pain. Scand J Rehab Med 1989; 21:81-95. 1990; 22:181-194.

10. Hazard RG et al 1989 Functional restoration with behavioural support. A one year prospective study of patients with chronic low back pain. Spine 14:157-161.

11. Kane RL et al 1974 Manipulating the patient: A comparison of the effectiveness of physician and chiropractor care. Lancet 1333-1336.

12. Koes BW et al 1992 Randomised clinical trial of manipulative therapy and physiotherapy for persistent back and neck complaints: results of one year follow up. Brit Med J 304:601-605.

13. Lindstrom I et al 1992 Mobility, strength and fitness after a graded activity program for patients with subacute low back pain. Spine 17:641-652.

14. Linton JJ et al 1993 controlled study of the effects of an early intervention on acute musculoskeletal pain problems. Pain 54:353-359.

15. Manniche C et al 1988 Clinical trial of intensive muscle training for chronic low back pain. Lancet 1473-6.

16. Mayer TG et al 1987 A prospective two year study of functional restoration in industrial low back injury. An objective assessment procedure. JAMA 258:1763-1767.

17. Meade TW et al 1990 Low back pain of mechanical origin: randomised comparison of chiropractic and hospital outpatient treatment. Brit Med J 300:1431-1437.

18. Mitchell RI, Carmen GM, 1990 Results of a multicenter trial using an intensive active exercise program for the treatment of acute soft tissue and back injuries. Spine 15:514-521.

19. Oland G Tveiten G 1991 A trial of modern rehabilitation for chronic low-back pain and disability: vocational outcome and effect of pain modulation. Spine 16:457-459.

20. Royal College of Radiologists, Making the best use of a department of radiology: guidelines for doctors. Second edition 1993.

21. Sachs BL et al 1990 Spinal rehabilitation by work tolerance based on objective physical capacity assessment of dysfunction. Spine 15:1325-1332.

22. Wiesel SW et al 1988 Evaluation and outcome of low-back pain of unknown etiology. Spine 13:679-680.

Appendix H References to CASG Back Pain Report

AHCPR 1994 Agency for Health Care Policy and Research, US Department of Health and Human Services. Management Guidelines for acute low back pain.

Allan D B, Waddell G 1989 An historical perspective on low back pain and disability. Acta Orthop Scand Suppl 234 60:1-23

Cherkin DC, Deyo RA, 1993 Non-surgical hospitalisation for low-back pain: is it necessary? Spine 18:1728-1735.

Croft P, et al 1994 Low back pain in the community and in hospitals. A report to the Clinical Standards Advisory Group. Prepared by the Arthritis & Rheumatism Council, Epidemiology Research Unit, University of Manchester

Dept of Health 1992 The Health of the Nation: a strategy for health in England. HMSO

DHSS 1979 Working group on back pain. HMSO

Fordyce W E, et al 1994 Pain in the workforce: management of disability in non-specific low back pain. A report of a task force of the International Association for the Study of Pain

Haldeman S, Rubinstein S M, 1992 Cauda equina syndrome in patients undergoing manipulation of the lumbar spine. Spine 17:1469-1473

Halpin S F S, et al, 1991 Radiographic examination of the lumbar spine in a community: an audit of current practice. Brit Med J 303:813-815

Jette A M et al 1994 Physical therapy episodes of care for patients with low back pain Phys Ther 74:101-110

Koes B W, et al 1991 Physiotherapy exercises and back pain: a blinded review. Brit Med J 302:1572-1576

Moffett J K, Richardson G, Maynard A 1993 Back pain: what is its impact on society?-Report to the Department of Health from the Centre for Health Economics, University of York

NHS 1993 Clinical effectiveness NHS ME EL(93)115

NHS and Community Care Act 1990

Office of Health Economics 1985 Back Pain. London

OPCS 1993 Hickman,M,Mason,V, The prevalence of back pain. A report prepared for the Dept of Health by the Office of Population Censuses and Surveys, Social Survey Division, based on the Omnibus Survey March, Apr, June 1993,

Roland M, Dixon M 1989 The role of an educational booklet in managing patients presenting with back pain in primary care. In Roland M Jenner J (Eds) Back pain: new approaches to education and rehabilitation, Manchester Univ

Royal College of Radiologists, 1993 Making the best use of a department of radiology: guidelines for doctors. Second Edition.

Scottish Office 1993 Clinical guidelines. A report by a working group set up by the Clinical Resources and Audit Group

Scottish Office 1994 The management of patients with chronic pain. Report of a working group of the National Medical Advisory Committee (draft).

Spitzer W O, et al 1987 Scientific approach to the assessment and management of activity-related spinal disorders. A monograph for clinicians. Report of the Quebec Task Force on spinal disorders. Spine 12 Suppl 1: S1-S59

Waddell G 1993 Simple low back pain: rest or active exercise? Ann Rheum Dis 52:317-319.

Waddell G, Bryn-Jones M 1993 British sickness and invalidity benefit for back incapacities: 1953-54 to 1991-92. Unpublished data prepared for the National Back Pain Association and CSAG.

Walsh K, et al 1992 Low back pain in eight areas of Britain J Epidem Comm Health 46: 227-230.

Welsh Office NHS Directorate 1992 Protocol for investment in health gain: pain, discomfort and palliative care.

CSAG report on back pain– Government response

1.   The Government welcomes the Clinical Standards Advisory Group's Report on Back Pain which has drawn on a considerable body of research evidence and clinical experience. Particularly welcome is CSAG's finding (paragraph 4.26 of the Report) that the NHS reforms are in general stimulating new and improved services for acute back pain.

2.   We note that CSAG has focused particularly on the management of low back pain in the first six months and the prevention of chronic disability and that CSAG is seeking what the Chairman of its Back Pain Committee, Professor Michael Rosen, has described as a "revolution" in the early treatment of back pain. The central core of CSAG's recommendations is that changes are necessary both in the timing and nature of clinical intervention on the premise that earlier and more effective treatment can prevent back pain becoming chronic. Clearly this outcome, if it can be achieved, would be highly desirable. CSAG's view that its recommendations are cost-neutral is welcome and no doubt purchasing authorities will take this into account.

3.   Although founded on research evidence on what interventions are effective the management guidelines proposed by the CSAG, and their implications for service arrangements and resources, have not been tested in this country. Nevertheless, there are indications that much of the current action on back pain is relatively ineffective, and adoption of the CSAG management guidelines would reduce this.

4.   CSAG has recommended that the NHS and the Health Departments should evaluate integrated primary care for the management of back pain. As part of the NHS research and development programme the Standing Group on Health Technology Assessment (SGHTA) has identified a number of priorities for research which include work on back pain, in particular low back pain surgery, effectiveness of physiotherapy and imaging in the management of low back pain. A study is currently being commissioned on the evaluation of routine referrals for x-rays of patients presenting to GPs with low back pain.

5.   A joint Department of Health-Medical Research Council (MRC) working party is being set up to consider the feasibility and potential benefits of research on the SGHTA priorities concerning back pain and to advise on other research priorities in this area. The CSAG recommendations for research will be put to the joint DH-MRC working group.

6.   The CSAG Report has documented the significant problem that low back pain causes for patients, the NHS and society as a whole in its effects on capacity for work. We believe that valuable changes can be made founded on the CSAG's recommendations. We therefore look to clinicians and NHS managers to consider in the light of this report what action they could usefully take. Educational material for patients with simple back pain and the general public might form an element of such action.

7.   As is normal practice with CSAG reports, copies will be distributed to purchasing authorities (including Family Health Services Authorities) and to provider hospitals, and to the relevant professional and educational organisations. In the context of the clinical effectiveness programme the report is being drawn to the attention of the NHS as a useful source of information.

8.   Back pain has already been identified in the Health of the Nation White Paper as among those strong candidates for Key Area status where the Government believes that further development and research is necessary before national targets can be set. The position will be kept under review.

9.   The Department of Health has already acted on the recommendation that the report should be discussed with the Department of Social Security by involving that Department in preliminary discussions and in the formulation of this Government Response. Such discussions will continue as necessary though it should be noted that benefit matters are entirely for DSS.

10.   Fiscal policy is outside the remit of CSAG and an argument for change is not demonstrated.

11.   We feel it would be premature to comment at this stage on recommendations on the detail of service provision which may be the subject of further research investigation. We do however commend them for consideration and we will take note of emerging views, as well as relevant research findings and the resource implications of any change, in considering any further action which it might be appropriate to take centrally.